THE GPS PARADIGM

FOR SUCCESSFUL MERGERS, ACQUISITIONS & JOINT VENTURES

The Definitive Inorganic Growth Playbook
for Business Founders, Leaders, Bankers, Finance Heads,
Legal Professionals and Students

NITIN POTDAR

INDIA • SINGAPORE • MALAYSIA

Notion Press

No.8, 3rd Cross Street
CIT Colony, Mylapore
Chennai, Tamil Nadu – 600004

First Published by Notion Press 2021
Copyright © Nitin Potdar 2021
All Rights Reserved.

ISBN 978-1-63832-574-1

This book has been published with all efforts taken to make the material error-free after the consent of the author. However, the author and the publisher do not assume and hereby disclaim any liability to any party for any loss, damage, or disruption caused by errors or omissions, whether such errors or omissions result from negligence, accident, or any other cause.

While every effort has been made to avoid any mistake or omission, this publication is being sold on the condition and understanding that neither the author nor the publishers or printers would be liable in any manner to any person by reason of any mistake or omission in this publication or for any action taken or omitted to be taken or advice rendered or accepted on the basis of this work. For any defect in printing or binding the publishers will be liable only to replace the defective copy by another copy of this work then available.

Synopsis

This is the first book of its kind, which prescribes a far-sighted scientific theory—the GPS Paradigm for M&As and JVs—to enable companies across sectors and spheres to thrive (not merely survive), stay relevant, and ensure sustainable growth. It enables and empowers founders, business leaders, CEOs and professionals, including investment bankers, lawyers and tax advisors across different generations and businesses to steer their future business voyages and expeditions. Simply put, this book is for those mavericks who, more than merely driving the change, are aspiring to be the change.

> "Corporate Restructuring read with GPS Paradigm – a Gateway to Survival and Growth"
>
> – Dr. K. R. Chandratre Former President, ICSI

> "This is a treasure trove of experiential insights and surgical recommendations, a bible for budding corporate lawyers, M & A aspirants in particular."
>
> – Ramanjun Mukherjee Founder LawSikho

> "This book provides all the ammunition for enhancing the end to end decision making specific to M&As and JVs. I absolutely recommend it to the inhouse counsel fraternity at large."
>
> – Deepak Acharya, General Counsel, Wipro

Dedicated to all those who work towards (or think of) making the planet a beautiful place to live in...

Contents

Foreword 9

Preface 11

Chapter 1   **Envisioning the Future of Mergers & Acquisitions and Joint Ventures** 15

    1. Unfolding the GPS Paradigm 20

    2. Ground Intelligence 21

    3. Unconventional Partnerships 22

    4. Strategic Solutions 23

    5. GPS Paradigm and Technology......................24

    6. M&As and JVs Compared – A Closer Look at Growth Strategies 29

    7. The GPS Paradigm: Tailor-Made for Growth – Whether M&As or JVs.....................31

Chapter 2   **Unfolding the M&A Core** 33

    1. M&A Phraseology and Types of Mergers 34

    2. Acquisitions 38

    3. Purpose of Any Acquisition 39

      4. Legal Due Diligence 41

      5. Indian Jurisprudence on Critical
         M&A Components 44

**Chapter 3 Institutionalizing M&A Capabilities:
Need of the Hour 61**

      1. Implementation of M&A as a Business Strategy 63

      2. Competition and Valuation in Tech-Centric
         M&A Deals 69

      3. Brand Value and the GPS Paradigm 74

      4. HR and the GPS Paradigm 75

Chapter 4 Unleashing the M&A Force 83

      1. Ground Intelligence for M&As 83

      2. Unconventional Partnerships in M&A 86

      3. Strategic Solutions for M&As 88

      4. GPS Paradigm in Practice for M&As 89

      5. GPS Paradigm Triumphs: Sterling Examples of
         Leading Tech-Giants 92

Chapter 5 Historical Trajectory of M&A 109

Chapter 6 Classic M&A Transactions at a Glance 115

Chapter 7 Unfolding the JV Core 119

      1. JVs and the 1991 Economic
         Liberalization in India 120

      2. Structuring Joint Ventures 123

Chapter 8 Unleashing the JV Force 151

      1. Joint Ventures 151

      2. GPS Paradigm in JVs 154

      3. Classic JVs 161

Chapter 9 My Tryst with M&As and JVs 167

Foreword

Nitin Potdar has given the global M&A community an invaluable gift in book form, a must-have for every library. The awesome depth of his research – both global and domestic – is rare and most refreshing. Nitin's technical and regulatory insights, supremely relevant quotes and his wealth of experiential learning lend unique colour and texture to this book. Every thought is well-illustrated and conveyed in a simple and lucid language.

Nitin has also shared the fascinating trials and triumphs of his life—generously and transparently—with his readers. Those like me, who deeply value his comradeship, will be thrilled to rediscover his inimitably amiable persona interspersed in the pages of this book.

In every aspect of life, data-led decisions are fast becoming the evolving norms of a 'new normal'. Nitin's GPS Paradigm is a unique reinforcement of this fact for the business world, a potent and purposeful convergence of ground-level intelligence, unique partnerships, and strategic solutions. Every key stakeholder of the ensuing worldwide upheavals that will in turn create new ecosystems will benefit from a careful absorption of the GPS idea whose time has come!

In a post-COVID-19 era, this book will serve as a universal toolkit for M&As and JVs: a dependable, robust, practical, and immensely energizing master algorithm for achieving measurable and sustainable business success in a world thriving on disruptive innovation.

I highly recommend this book to every person working on corporate growth strategies, including M&As, JVs and collaborations.

– **Shailesh Haribhakti**
Chartered Accountant

* * *

Preface

The year 2020 was the Year of Global Lockdowns: when the entire world suffered a deep freeze by the lethal blows of a microorganism called the coronavirus, not for a day, week, or month but a whole year! In fact, even as I write this preface, the threat of a partial lockdown yet looms large.

Having said that, amid the disruption caused by sealed geographical borders and an uncertain economic future, a bigger disruption is at play, and that too at a furious pace: the disruption of technological innovation, a perpetual disruption which has made 'thinking beyond the normal' the 'new normal'.

For many new-age innovators with disruptive innovation embedded in their DNA, this is a godsend for mapping their growth path. On the other hand, most established business leaders and veteran decision makers are grappling with a binary choice: either pursue greener pastures rooted in technological integration or face a bleak future of roadblocks and downfalls.

I recollect the wise words of Uday Kotak, founder and executive vice chairman of Kotak Mahindra Bank in the context of technological innovation: "I am excited, but very challenged. I keep wondering at night: 'Will I have a bank the next morning, or will some technology company be doing banking without needing a bank?'"

For a person like me, who has traversed a long winding route – from pre-information technology age, introspection about the essence and credence of future technologies was long overdue and the forced sabbatical due to the lockdown since March 2020 provided the proverbial trigger. As providence would have it, I read 'Jonathan Livingston Seagull' during this time, a book written by pilot-turned-barnstormer-turned-celebrated author Richard Bach, about a story that tells us not to believe our eyes—as they show limitations, but to look with our understanding, find out what we already know, and learn the way to fly. I read Jonathan Seagull several times and each time my subconscious mind flashed with memories of my school – college – law education – internship – solicitors' exam – early days of law practice – my failures – dejection – anxieties – my mentors – seniors – law firms where I worked – top clients – and my extensive professional working experience of structuring several M&As and JVs!

What struck me the most was the urgent need to share my scientific theory titled 'GPS Paradigm' for M&As and JVs, a way forward to effectively deal with the diktats of disruptive technology and perpetual unpredictability. I have recommended an end-to-end solution model to enable every company to thrive (not merely survive), stay relevant, and ensure sustainable growth and be aspirational.

The GPS Paradigm represents three interwoven prerequisites. One, the acquisition of Ground Intelligence before undertaking any M&A or initiation of JV talks; two, the need to foster Unconventional Partnerships; and three, the design and delivery of Strategic Solutions. G stands for 'Ground intelligence', P for 'Partnerships' rooted in unconventionality, and S stands for 'Strategic Solutions'. The GPS at play is a unique, wholesome Global Positioning System that helps companies with landscape navigation, astute collaboration, and sustainable progression in the same breath.

The tenets of the GPS Paradigm for M&As and JVs are based on the length, breadth, and width of over three decades of my experiences and insights, as also several deep dive conversations with CEOs, CFOs, legal advisors and counsel, among other stakeholders across different domains, industries, and countries. The GPS Paradigm offers a totally new way of looking at M&As and JVs for business founders, leaders, CEOs, bankers, finance heads, legal professionals, and students to fulfil their aspirational goals. In my view the GPS Paradigm applies to all types of M&As and JVs (in all variants) across all industries and service sectors.

I have also shared my professional journey in the same book for two reasons: (a) to articulate the theory of GPS Paradigm citing my experiences and (b) to provide career insights for law students & in-house counsel who wish to pursue M&A or Joint Venture practice. On this count, I have explicitly shared practical tips – a to-do-list for them to become M&A lawyers.

Before closing I must thank my associate, Jashan Merchant, who helped me with the extensive research for this book.

Whilst my journey continues, I sincerely hope that the theory of GPS Paradigm that I have elaborately set out in this book would prove useful to all mavericks who, more than merely driving the change, **are aspiring to be the change!**

Sincerely yours
– **Nitin Potdar**
nitinpotdar@yahoo.com

* * *

www.nitinpotdar.com

Chapter 1

Envisioning the Future of Mergers & Acquisitions and Joint Ventures

In a 2010 media interview, on the eve of the 40th anniversary of his celebrated book **Future Shock**, Alvin Toffler made a very incisive observation:

In the past, you made a decision and that was it. Now, you make a decision, and you say, 'What happens next?' There's always a next.

This Toffler quote aptly sums up the world we are living in, a world of ceaseless change and infinite possibilities. The premise of his book *Future Shock* – that precipitous and rapid change tends to disorient people – has become more relevant than ever before, given the far-reaching impact caused by the protracted COVID-19 pandemic. Toffler was equally prophetic in another epic work, **Third Wave,** where he exposed the fundamental flaw of building a new structure from scratch without grasping the deep-rooted upheavals of phenomenal disruptions.

Toffler's *Third Wave* observation applies in toto to the digital revolution that is way more elusive than what meets the eye. Any generalization or sweeping suppositions would be rendered futile in a forgone conclusion—such is the speed, velocity, and acceleration of this fourth wave of unprecedented change and transformation. Its magnitude and density are yet unknown, what's known though is the acute need for a highly collaborative and integrated effort of key business stakeholders to script measurable and sustainable success stories in a foggy environment marked by unnerving uncertainty.

The coming age, beyond doubt, will be replete with global uncertainties, rapid technological breakthroughs and successive paradigm shifts rooted in disruptive innovation. The impending wave of unprecedented change and transformation is unnerving, to say the least. Going forward, business stakeholders – both established and emerging – will have to necessarily go deep to secure ground intelligence and strike unconventional partnerships and create potent collaborations for developing strategic solutions in the respective spheres and sectors.

In a business world engulfed by technological advancements, industry champions can't afford to be unaware of the essence and credence of the reigning trends – whether cloud-enabled infrastructures, AI-powered applications, or hyperautomation-led operations. They would have to wilfully embrace a *dynamic-by-default* business environment defined by remote working, contactless deliveries, and micro mobility solutions, as also put the all-pervasive technology paradigms into practice – whether effecting key customer service enhancements through micro-moments, enhancing key business decisions and resolving sticky market challenges with big data analytics and quantum computing, carrying out product improvements through IoT and nanotechnology, initiating digitalization and blockchain-led supply chain efficiencies, or transforming manufacturing and operational systems with the help of collaborative robots or cobots, drones, aerial birds, and additive manufacturing. These defining paradigms would no longer remain buzzwords for posterity, but become business anthems for achieving a real-time production and productivity boost, here and now!

Consequently, the gen-next business leaders would have to be extra vigilant about change and transformation, as also extra considerate about surviving the inevitable consequences of sudden disruptions (COVID-19 is a case in point). At the same time, they must be confident about their Mergers & Acquisitions (M&As) and Joint Venture (JVs) plans and strategies, soaring on the wings of unflinching conviction, dogged determination and calculated risk-taking. Future leaders would need to demonstrate the foresight of a true visionary leader, making the most of the real-time data available on their fingertips.

GPS Paradigm

The best way to predict the future...is to invent it.

– Alan Kay, Computer scientist

This is the first book of its kind which prescribes a far-sighted scientific theory which I have christened as the GPS Paradigm for M&As and JVs, an end-to-end systemic solution to enable every company to thrive (not merely survive), stay relevant, and ensure sustainable growth. I prescribe this theory based on the length, breadth and width of my professional experience of several transactions over three decades, including innumerable deep dive conversations with business founders, leaders, CEOs, CFOs, bankers, finance professionals, legal advisors and in-house counsel among other stakeholders across different domains, industries, and countries.

Mergers, acquisitions and joint ventures are undoubtedly the key growth strategies helping corporates achieve diverse goals—whether diversification, consolidation, gaining market shares, conquering new geographies, incorporating new products and services, or securing new methods, skills and competencies. The choice of nomenclature, in a few cases, may be dictated by reasons rooted in political correctness—for example a stated merger may actually be an acquisition to circumvent the negative connotation of the latter term—but the fact remains that mergers and acquisitions have far-reaching consequences for the partnering firms and their communities. They not only impact the ownership patterns and valuations; they also deeply affect people, work cultures and markets.

That's precisely why it is extremely important that both M&As and JVs must be done right. Sadly, the reality is discernibly depressing. The failure rate of M&As, as per several studies, is anywhere between 70% to 90%. The prime reasons for this dismal outcome include 1) flawed distinction between strategic intent and operational objectives, 2) weak leadership, 3) erroneous or loosely coupled integrations, 4) inadequate attention to people and culture issues, and 5) unscientific valuations and value propositions.

Notwithstanding the high failure rate, the advent of breakthrough technologies has necessitated new business models in manufacturing or service sectors across different industries and geographies. In the new regime, 'customer' and their preferences would form the epicenter of any corporate growth mandate, not valuations, cash profits or other motives. Going forward, M&As and JVs would be the defining strategic solution frameworks, not just for achieving aspirational growth but even for the sheer survival of many organisations. This dictum makes the theory of GPS Paradigm for M&As and JVs inevitably essential.

Hence, I have tried to include the basics or fundamentals of M&A and JVs in the chapters 'M&A Core' and 'JV Core' to emphasize that the GPS Paradigm cuts across all concepts and models of business combination and growth with the help of classic examples.

I believe that the ongoing flurry of M&As and JVs are the outcome of increased deregulation, globalization, and selective liberalization adopted by several countries the world over. I strongly sense the need for a more scientific and structured approach to deal with the exponentially growing dominance of future technologies (of which many are in nascent stages of development). I expect the GPS Paradigm to provide the requisite approach and methodologies to enable companies to ride the wave of disruptive technologies amid the uncertainties surrounding their business. Firm traces of the GPS Paradigm can be found in the recent sterling examples of several M&As and JVs structured by the leading tech giants like Facebook, Google, Amazon and Jio, and other companies cited in this book. I sincerely hope that this book helps founders, business leaders, CEOs, and professionals including investment bankers, lawyers and tax advisors across different generations and businesses, to understand and apply the tenets of the GPS Paradigm in their future business voyages and expeditions. **This book is for those mavericks who, more than merely driving the change, are aspiring to be the change.**

Having worked with many start-ups across different sectors, I reckon that 'thinking beyond the normal' is the new normal for the new generation; the craving to be offbeat is in their DNA. No wonder, all technology themes like 'disruptive', 'innovative', and 'breakthrough' are anthems for them. The GPS Paradigm is the normal way of 'doing businesses for them, albeit largely in bits and pieces.

Powered by robust search engines, incisive AI algorithms, and foolproof data analysis, they are organically adept at acquiring real time 'ground intelligence', which in turn keeps them on the constant lookout for 'unconventional partnerships' that help deliver 'strategic solutions'. In sharp contrast, a majority of traditional business founders and leaders seem to be grappling with the basics of rudimentary technologies, leave alone AI, robotics, data analytics or blockchain. For them, technology is merely a high-tech 'gadget' to support business, not a key enabler. **For the Start-up Millennials and Gen Z fraternity, technology is synonymous with doing business, which is evident from the plethora of revenue models that have emerged in the last couple of years, on the cusp of gen-next technologies and unconventional partnerships.**

The GPS Paradigm is not a formula for blind adoption, nor is it a silver bullet for all ills. Business by its very nature is prone to transactional failures despite the best of intentions, but more importantly, even the transient failures won't in the least disprove the tenets and principles of the **GPS Paradigm**; instead, they would only reinforce the unshakable doctrines—such is the fidelity and foolproofness of this paradigm.

Historically, many companies may have unknowingly followed the **GPS Paradigm** principles; those who did reaped the rewards in full measure. Going forward, however, the **GPS Paradigm** alone will help corporates make the most of the global growth opportunities, as also counter the umpteen challenges lurking in the background. To help understand why, it is essential to put the **GPS Paradigm** in perspective.

1. Unfolding the GPS Paradigm

Adherence to the rock-solid tenets of the GPS Paradigm for M&As and JVs alone will help companies not only survive the unforeseen existential crises but also emerge as a thriving force in the future.

So, what exactly is the GPS Paradigm for M&As and JVs and why do I call it so? GPS represents three interwoven prerequisites. One, the acquisition of **ground intelligence** before undertaking any M&A or initiation of JVs talks; two, the need to foster **unconventional partnerships;** and three, the design and delivery of **strategic solutions.** G stands for **Ground intelligence,** P stands for **Partnerships rooted in unconventionality**, and S stands for **Strategic solutions.**

The GPS Paradigm, by virtue of the synergistic play of each of the G, P, and S components, helps organizations across sectors and spheres discover and study key global paradigms (both existing and evolving), establish their own growth coordinates, and chart their progression through potent growth strategies like organic expansions, M&A, and JVs. The GPS at play is a unique, wholesome **Global Positioning System** that helps companies with landscape navigation, astute collaboration, and sustainable progression in the same breath.

Unconventional Partnerships

Ground intelligence **Strategic solutions**

[The GPS Paradigm visual shows the three components of Ground Intelligence, Unconventional Partnerships, and Strategic Solutions as interlaced Borromean rings. Named after the Italian House of Borromeo, these rings represent a fortified unity that best depicts the inseparability and integrity of the GPS Paradigm.]

To capture the soul of the GPS paradigm, it is imperative to capture the essence of the **G, P,** and **S** components that stretch way beyond their dictionary meanings and **work in unison, not in isolation,** to help corporates across different spheres and sectors create measurable and sustainable business value and a unique competitive edge.

Let us dive deeper into the mesmerizing depths of each of these intertwined components:

2. Ground Intelligence

Intelligence, at its inclusive best, implies several attributes: the capability to learn and absorb facts, truths, phenomena and concepts, adaptability to quickly address circumstantial and environmental demands, capacity for acquiring emotional knowledge and demonstrating conscious creativity, and even higher-level abilities like critical thinking, abstract reasoning, mental representation, problem solving, and decision making.

The G of the GPS Paradigm is about being rooted to the ground in a more ingrained fashion that what the military connotation would imply.

However, the term 'ground intelligence' finds its roots in military parlance, implying the key function of planning and steering the deployment of ground reconnaissance units, thereby encompassing analysis, evaluation, and estimation of operational situations imperative for the formulation, coordination, and execution of appropriate strategies.

Today, a firm cannot get its business growth plans off the ground in the real sense unless it intelligently studies and analyses the contextual ground realities across the globe, not just the actualities limited to local geographies.

How did the ones before us approach this decision? What were the learnings from their trials and triumphs? Do I look at immediate top-line possibilities or should I focus on long-term bottom line prospects? Why should I bother about environmental, social and governance norms while planning my progression? What works and if yes how long, what does not and why? Answers to these crucial questions will only come from ground intelligence. In the context of M&As and JVs, ground intelligence is not just securing key information about the target company, or competitors, or brands but also about cultivating the holistic acumen to be able to envision a sustainable future based on the extrapolation of the actionable base information.

3. Unconventional Partnerships

The P of GPS puts a premium on unconventionality only because the modern-day business would demand it upfront.

The dictionary meaning of the word 'unconventional' is anything that is not based on or conforming to what is generally done or believed. However, the unconventionality of P of the GPS Paradigm does not prescribe 'out of the ordinary' thought and action for the sake of it. Like how a diversion is required only when the straight road is blocked for some reason, the GPS Paradigm advocates unconventionality when the conventions do not work or do not take you to the desired destination. Having said that, **in the impending technology-led era, conventional routes will invariably face a litmus test at every turn and a twist on every run, which is why the GPS Paradigm stresses on unconventional partnerships that demand analyzing possibilities beyond plain vanilla contemplation.** To cite a simple instance for the sake of clarity, a boutique law firm, or a small creative agency, in their quest to expand reach or move up the market value chain, may end up partnering with an IT start-up or a nimble-footed tech crusader, given the promise of a wider reach, innovative services and 24x7 customer connect across diverse locations. The conventional route in this case would be to merge or tie up with another law or creative firm with different practice or greater repute and size. That explains the current trend of high-end travel companies seamlessly collaborating with smart set-ups from seemingly unrelated sectors like food, fashion, and ride-sharing players, solely led by their customer preferences.

4. Strategic Solutions

The S of the GPS Paradigm is set in motion in the context of solutions that promise sustainability, not merely success that can be transient and worse, even counterproductive beyond a point.

Before we come to solutions, let us focus on the word **strategy** which again has its genesis in military terminology and refers to a plan of action designed to achieve a particular goal as opposed to tactics which implies a plan of comparatively lesser significance. Let us again take a simple hypothetical case of a paper company eyeing a pencil manufacturer for synergistic growth. The foreseeable future seems bright, the pencil manufacturer has a robust business model, and the numbers as projected by the finance team are by far impressive. On the flip side is this huge uproar over the rampant use of wood for pencil production. It is reported that approximately 82,000 trees are cut down every year to make 14 billion traditional wooden pencils.

A strategic solution in this case would be to tie up with a mid-sized player manufacturing recycled paper pencils that eliminate the need for cutting down trees, and they decompose quickly causing minimal environmental pollution unlike wood and plastic pencils.

To take a more credible real-world example of sustainable success rooted in a strategic solution is the **Apple iPod** which foresaw the opportunity in the digital music space long before its competitors even imagined it. Focusing on the limitations of digital music players, the company diligently designed the iTunes-compatible iPod, diversifying far away from its core of computer and software manufacture, and the rest is history. The idea of direct music download was truly path-breaking and hence proved sustainable for a significantly long time. Even now, iPod Touch offers the virtues of a handy device with easy functionality amid the maze of high-end Apple products, serving the needs of a niche segment – kids and elders.

5. GPS Paradigm and Technology

Disruptive technology is a sword hanging over every modern-day company, and the GPS Paradigm makes it an integral part of the M&As or JVs strategy over and above presupposing the standardization and incorporation of critical elements like due diligence (financial, legal, environmental, technical, and reputational), documentation, and regulatory approvals.

Evolution of Revolutions

The GPS Paradigm for M&As or JVs thrives on disruptive technology as it has all the levers to make the most of the given opportunities in a fluidic business environment of fast-evolving paradigms and technological innovations.

It is prudent and pertinent to draw a few parallels between the first-ever industrial revolution and the ongoing digital revolution. If steam fuelled the bygone Industrial Revolution, data is powering the modern-day digital revolution. In the specific context of M&As or JVs and the GPS Paradigm, we need to focus on the striking similarities and stark differences between the industrial revolution and the digital revolution.

Let's briefly recount the M&As and JVs during the first industrial revolution. As explained in later sections, the revolution had a twin effect on business and industry: while most struggling firms predictably met the fate of unceremonious closure, several manufacturing players with grit, gumption, vision, and conviction became part of a humungous consolidation drive. Comprised chiefly of **horizontal mergers**, this amalgamation spree ensured economic prosperity and burgeoning competition, and booming capital markets, while boosting mass production and extended distribution of goods led by technological breakthroughs and better rail, road, and telegraphic infrastructure. Of course, the massive churn had its share of turbulence and turmoil too, what with heavy market speculation, some instances of suspect M&As motives, and growing public resentment over the unequal wealth distribution and apparent government apathy.

Coming back to our moot point, there's a thread of commonality that binds the two revolutions of altogether different eras: the first industrial revolution and the present-day digital revolution, popularly called the Industry 4.0. Both phases have been marked by unprecedented change – whether technological or organizational, the outcome of which has been a mixed bag: cutting-edge technology, high liquidity, big-ticket investments, massive production surge, significant cost reduction and globally expanding markets on the one hand, and superfluous production capacities, dropping labour incomes, and growing wage cuts and job losses on the other. Both revolutions have

Given the relative predictability of this era, the GPS Paradigm was not a compelling need (although there are several instances where visionary firms applied it both knowingly and unknowingly and reaped the rewards).

forced conventional players to adapt to the fast-evolving industry and market paradigms through synergistic alliances and tech-led forays into sunrise areas.

Notwithstanding the similarities, there are a few traits exclusive to the digital revolution which merit careful observation. Common to all the differentiators of the digital revolution is the maddening velocity at which change is happening all around us. The change during the first industrial revolution was overwhelming no doubt, but there was a ring of predictability around it – how manufacturing facilities would be enhanced, how machines will operate, how markets would respond, how demand would grow, how competitive edge would be created, and so on and so forth. The biggest impact was psychological, given the rather ruthless manner in which people suited to an agrarian way of life were suddenly forced to grapple with machines on a shop floor.

A firm did not necessarily have to gather meticulous bits of ground intelligence; it did not have to be necessarily unconventional in forming alliances, nor did it have to be dutifully strategic about its solution making, especially if its size and scope was limited to specific geographies. Firms could survive and thrive with consciously constricted ambitions in niche markets.

Disruption today has become the ruling norm for business sustainability, and the new paradigm is relevant only until the next wave is ushered in. Today, the single-most key driver of this furious transformation is the advent of technology.

However, now change is necessarily fast and furious, and corporate aspirations are invariably global. The ubiquity and digital reach of marketing channels, and the sheer volatility of customer trends and preferences mean that production and productivity targets need to be wildly flexible. What held true sometime back can be rendered hopelessly redundant within days. It would be pertinent to note one, the crux of modern-day technology, and two, its impact on business and industry today, tomorrow, and beyond.

1. Crux of Modern-Day Technology

> *As each wave of technology is released, it must be accompanied by a demand for new skills, new language. Consumers must constantly update their ways of thinking, always questioning their understanding of the world. Going back to old ways, old technology is forbidden. There is no past, no present, only an endless future of inadequacy.*
>
> *– Richard Kadrey, Novelist*

Yes, not only is technology in the current era inherently disruptive, leading the industry 4.0 strides from the front, it ceaselessly threatens us with a future of inadequacy, urging us to deal with it in real time. Artificial intelligence has already seeped into the very core of business and industry, enriched by the humungous data deluge and vast computing power. Given the velocity at which disruptive innovation is transforming the business world across industries, technology is not merely a key enabler now, but a key driver. In fact, going forward, many M&As and JVs would largely hinge on the competency of the stakeholders to fathom the intricacies of machine learning and advanced data analytics.

Beyond doubt, technology has democratized the business arena given the fact that new, agile start-ups with potent tech-enabled platforms can today dethrone renowned veterans in quick time, thanks to their disruptive solutions of measurable and sustainable value. The market side push is equally vicious today as novel tech-powered forms and vehicles of consumer engagement coupled with fast-changing consumer behaviour impact the design and delivery of products and services in close to real time.

2. Impact on Business and Industry

In light of the dramatic changes brought about by the deep technologies – artificial intelligence, robotics, internet of things, block chain, cyber security, and big data, it is my belief that those organizations that are not Fourth Industrial Revolution ready are going to see a dramatic change in the value and valuation of their company.

– Danil Kerimi, Digital Transformation Expert

Several experts have time and again stressed on key measures to help companies approach the tech challenges of the fourth industrial revolution. Among other things, it is important for founders and CEOs to continuously seek tech-enabled innovation both within and outside the four walls of their enterprises. Merely relying on in-house competencies and R&D explorations may not yield desired outcomes as fast as the market demands it. **The time to market is as important as the innovation itself, which is why inorganic growth through M&As or the JVs route becomes inevitable.** More importantly, the modern-day M&As or JVs would need to be strategic, looking beyond the low-hanging fruits of the short term and embedding crucial considerations like cultural fitment into their business decisions. They should envision the collaborative transformations of the acquirer and the acquired, judiciously blending the existing and emerging competencies of both, which can alone be achieved through seamless integration.

In the single-minded focus on the desired objectives, a firm should not lose sight of the peripheral opportunities for growth. This dual focus merits a good amount of experimentation and calculated risks based on authentic ground research. **Since success can't be guaranteed in this highly fluidic environment, calculated trial and error is a prudent ploy to try out a handful of potentially rewarding alternatives before freezing on a chosen few.** But this experimentation calls for holistic thinking and foresight. **It merits a comprehensive analysis of a wider** set of potential growth opportunities for separating the potential 'disruptions' from the mere 'eruptions'.

The need of the hour is for companies to apply the GPS Paradigm towards becoming the indisputable leaders of this digital revolution as part of their business strategy driven by M&As or forming JVs for strategic solutions whether in B2B or B2C.

I strongly believe that the **GPS Paradigm** would fast gain relevance as it provides a three-pronged foolproof strategy to help companies counter the threat and address the challenges of disruptive technology. By acquiring **ground intelligence**, companies can identify upcoming trends not only in the context of technology and innovation but also to make smart product tweaks in line with fast changing consumer preferences. Further, by being more than ready to forge **unconventional partnerships**, they can address the shifting market diktats better than what they can hope to achieve in isolation. And last but not the least, armed with actionable synergies, they can enhance their competitive edge through **strategic solutions** aimed at better customer experience and engagement. Gone are the days of incremental additions or tweaking manufacturing, marketing, or research & development efforts in the light of actual experience.

6. M&As and JVs Compared – A Closer Look at Growth Strategies

Business existence or expansion, at its very core, necessitates collaboration and co-creation, whether among internal stakeholders or between external entities. When growth-led circumstances so demand, expansion may imply merging with, taking over, or joining hands with other businesses. Such mergers, acquisitions, joint ventures, alliances, and collaborations are invariably about achieving trade-offs: potential management tussles, staff conflicts and other integration issues on the one hand, and a host of benefits on the other, including more resources at command, better market reach, shared skills, astute risk mitigation, and the like.

Mergers & Acquisitions	Joint Ventures
Merger: Two entities combine to form a single company by relinquishing erstwhile stocks and issuing new company stock. Works best when combined entity is bound to maximize revenues and efficiencies, and minimize costs. **Acquisition:** One company takes over another, buyer owns the combined set-up, separate identity of the target is dissolved. It works best for addressing weak spots through the takeover of a firm strong in the said areas as the integration becomes seamless, being specific and surgical in essence. A careful evaluation of risk factors and ROI considerations is MUST to justify the cost of M&A which are invariably prohibitive.	**Joint venture:** A legal partnership between two or more companies to make a new entity for competitive advantage. The new entity has a separate board and management team, all chosen representatives of founding organizations. Ideal for cases where target's value prop of products and services makes perfect business sense, but the takeover of operational aspects is not justified. **Strategic alliance:** A form of partnership to make the most of respective core strengths. Agreement could be close-knit or open-ended with regular performance reviews. Other partnerships imply 'teaming up' for a common cause through an agreement. Ideal for cases where target has many 'overkill' components apart from the specific areas where integration is justified.

Selecting a particular model for collaborative growth is not a black-and-white decision. It merits an incredibly careful study of the similarities and differences between the two models, as also their significance and effectiveness in the specific context of the given business situation. To choose the best strategy for growth, one needs to undertake a comprehensive analysis of the 'as-is'

environment, performance, and future potential, including the transactional hazards of regulatory regime or tax burdens. Post that, it is time to evaluate options to zero in on the most feasible and productive 'to be' option.

7. The GPS Paradigm: Tailor-Made for Growth – Whether M&As or JVs

Given the pace of globalization and disruptive innovation, the future of M&As or JVs would be largely guided by the **GPS Paradigm**, which takes into account the three vital growth components in this tech-driven era: ground intelligence, unconventional partnerships, and strategic solutions.

As technology has made the future completely unpredictable, survival, nay sustainability, is not about waiting for things to happen but to envision sunrise possibilities and create potent combinations, aimed at taking a decisive lead in the respective industries and markets.

Business leaders have long been pursuing M&As, JVs, alliances, and collaborations for business restructuring initiatives laden with the promise of both forward and backward integration growth. Typically, the mission was to increase revenues by adding new products through focused R&D, superior marketing, value-added manufacturing and use of cutting-edge technology. **Going forward, this conventional approach would have to pave the way for offbeat paradigms, given the disruptive innovation that has created new markets for novel products and more potent ways for market penetration and preferences.** As a result, business leaders depending on ground intelligence would have to scout for unconventional partners and offer strategic solutions, thereby seeking new commercial arrangements that go beyond conventional capital investments, brand licensing or royalties.

Social media, 3D manufacturing, e-commerce platforms, and other technological advancements would challenge and transform the typical M&As and JVs structures in unimaginable ways. The GPS Paradigm is our best bet to ride the tide in the new scheme of things.

M&As or JVs: Points to Note

- ✓ M&As are typically discussed at length – whether in corporate circles, analyst fraternity or media agencies. Every M&A invariably gets reported and the M&As of listed players are extensively analyzed and reported in terms of valuation, assets, business, technology, brands and even the swap ratio of shares. Joint Ventures are more of closed-door affairs; in fact, in many instances, the crux of crucial aspects of M&As may not be made public by choice.

- ✓ Globally, a M&A scheme invariably undergoes a detailed scrutiny by (a) the Board of Directors of respective companies (separate confirmation/opinion from Independent directors in case of listed companies), (b) shareholders, (c) lenders, (d) industry regulators and (e) court/antitrust regulators in some countries (Competition Commission in India). Such a comprehensive scrutiny and approval process is not followed while structuring a Joint Venture, save for approval of antitrust regulators, if and when required.

- ✓ Studying the hints provided by market response to plans of diversification or collaboration, as also operational and regulatory insights brought to light by past industry deals and are key to making a feasible decision.

- ✓ M&As imply exclusive control over the combined operations but come at a higher price tag besides call for owning up of all liabilities of the acquirer. JVs may not be that promising on the control front, but they are conclusively cost effective and more surgical in nature.

Chapter 2

Unfolding the M&A Core

The corporate and investment world invariably cheers the media announcement of any mega M&A deal with great enthusiasm! The news has an immediate impact on the stock prices. What also follows is a litany of loaded questions from all quarters, including valuation experts, analysts of equity swap ratios, regulators, industry veterans, and commentators. In my experience, big is not always beautiful when it comes to M&A transactions because of several inherent complexities. Having said that, size continues to attract maximum attention, and rightly so to a large extent. In India it is still a herculean challenge to structure large M&As within the permitted regulatory frame of the SEBI (Substantial Acquisition of Shares and Takeovers) Regulations, 2011 applied to listed companies. Also, large takeovers including hostile ones are still a distant dream due to the foreign exchange control regulations applicable to foreign investment in India.

There should be no doubt in the minds of business leaders and professionals that the GPS Paradigm will form the epicenter of ensuing evolution that a globalized, tech-driven business will undergo in future in any industry or service sector.

Mergers & Acquisitions is a robust, sophisticated, and well-legislated business tool in the hands of companies, which allows them to not only survive but grow and create value for all stakeholders, including founders, public shareholders, institutional investors, joint venture partners and business associates, employees, lenders and creditors, customers and suppliers, government, and communities. Fortunately, global legislative framework or the legal process for M&As allows companies to seamlessly (a) merge into one or more companies, (b) split into multiple independent companies (also known as demergers in India), (c) close down any non-core or unprofitable division while retaining focus on more profitable activity, (d) offer exit to any strategic partner or investor, including private equity, or (e) implement succession planning of family businesses across sectors (refer the section 'Indian Jurisprudence' of the next chapter).

Literally thousands of companies must have used or explored some form of M&A activity over time, with or without success. The objectives and considerations for each deal may differ depending upon the decision makers, industry, or geography, but the legal process or compliance is more or less the same across various jurisdictions, which till date has not deterred large or small companies from contemplating M&A activity. The GPS Paradigm helps them in their pursuit of future or aspirational growth. Fortunately, the key focus remains on integrity of data, transparency, and public interest.

The idea of touching the core of M&As and other business models is to clearly grasp how the GPS Paradigm cuts across the very structure and function of any business growth model, whether M&As or JVs. It is hence imperative that we study the key technical definitions, business concepts, historical perspectives, and jurisprudence of M&A and JVs before I highlight the need to institutionalize M&A and JV capabilities by virtue of the GPS Paradigm. This section is devoted to the M&A core.

1. M&A Phraseology and Types of Mergers

Merger Defined

Investopedia defines a merger as an agreement that combines two existing companies into one new company for a variety of reasons, including expansion of a company's reach, business segments and market share. Put differently, a merger is the voluntary fusion of two companies into one new legal entity on terms that are broadly equal. By virtue of a merger, two or more companies share resources towards achieving common objectives.

The prime motive of a merger is more often than not profit maximization, which may imply maximization of production, productivity, sale, market reach, and competitive edge. Another strong trigger for mergers is the need to establish synergies that result in acquisition of cutting-edge technologies, disruptive innovation, cost reduction and economies of scale.

In some cases, a merger may seek to address governance issues like weak or unprofessional management, or it may look at more potent ways to improve the image of the company, say by building a more commanding value proposition.

In order to appreciate this business tool and apply the GPS Paradigm to it, it would be prudent to examine various types of M&As that have evolved over a period of time, citing classic examples of each classification. I must mention here that the following definitions or classifications do not find place under Indian Companies Act, 2013 or the earlier Act of 1956.

a) **Conglomerate Merger:**

Meaning	A merger between two or more companies engaged in unrelated business activities, whether in different industries or different geographies, to create synergies aimed at enhancing value, performance, and economies of scale.
Salient points	A **pure conglomerate** involves two firms with zero commonality. A **mixed conglomerate** involves firms into unrelated business activities, seeking product or market extensions.

Continued...

	The biggest risk in a conglomerate merger is the immediate shift in business operations resulting from the merger, as the two companies operate in completely different markets and offer unrelated products/services.
	Companies with no overlapping factors will only merge if it makes sense from a shareholder's wealth perspective, that is, if the companies can create synergy, which includes enhancing value, performance, and cost savings.
Example	The Walt Disney Company merged with the American Broadcasting Company (ABC) in 1995.

b) Congeneric Merger:

Meaning	A combination of two or more companies operating in the same market or sector with overlapping factors like technology, and research and development. Also called 'Product Extension' merger.
Salient points	Combining product lines helps acquire a larger market share. The product lines are not same but related, utilizing similar distribution channels, production processes or supply chains.
Example	Citigroup's 1998 union with Travelers Insurance was a merger of two companies with complementing products.

c) Market Extension:

Meaning	Merger between companies selling the same products but competing in different markets.
Salient points	This merger also seeks to gain access to a bigger market and, thus, a bigger client base.
Example	Eagle Bancshares and RBC Centura merger in 2002.

d) Horizontal Merger:

Meaning	Merger between companies operating in the same industry.
Salient points	Common in industries with fewer firms, this merger seeks to create a larger business with greater market share, economies of scale and synergized operations, given the high competition among fewer players. The consequent market power surge may invite action under antitrust regulation.
Example	The 1998 merger of Daimler-Benz and Chrysler.

e) Vertical:

Meaning	Merger between two companies manufacturing components or providing services for a product merger.
Salient points	Companies within the same industry's supply chain combine their operations to increase synergies primarily through cost reduction. The purpose includes better quality control and seamless supply chain-wide information flow.
Example	The 2000 merger between Internet provider America Online (AOL) with media conglomerate Time Warner.

Often, mergers are also classified in terms of the following broad heads:

Business Combinations

Statutory Merger	The merged (or target) company ceases to exist. Acquirer assumes all merged assets and liabilities. Owners of merged companies often assume joint ownership of the merged set-up.
Subsidiary Merger	Acquired company becomes a subsidiary of the parent company. In a reverse subsidiary merger, a subsidiary of the acquiring company is merged into the target company.

Continued...

Consolidation	Two or more companies join to form a new company. In consolidation, combining firms have similar sizes unlike mergers which are marked by significant differences.
Reverse Merger	Acquiring company merges into the target company. Commonly happens when a company wishes to get publicly listed in a short span.
Mergers of Equals	Companies of similar sizes merge with each other.

Management-driven

Friendly Merger	Management of acquiring and target companies mutually and willingly agree to a takeover
Hostile Merger	Acquisition is against the will of the target management, often made via a dictatorial tender offer to the target company's shareholders.
Bailout M&As	Done to bail out sick companies or rehabilitate them according to schemes approved by financial institutions.

Geography-driven

Domestic Merger	Between two companies of the same nationality.
Cross-Border M&As	Also called international mergers, between two companies from different countries.

2. Acquisitions

Acquisitions are structured contractually in the form of transfer of business division on a going concern basis (also known as Slump Sale), share purchase transactions, or asset purchase (**tangibles** like plant or machinery or distribution, and **intangibles** like intellectual property comprising of brands/technology). Primarily, any M&A structure depends on the transaction tax advice, due diligence (legal, tax, technical, environmental, and reputational), and industry-specific regulatory approvals. The process gets a bit cumbersome in case of global business transfers involving assets of different geographies. In India, due to tax benefits or considerations, acquisitions are implemented via a court process as M&A transactions or demergers, even though it is tedious compared to a plain vanilla business transfer agreement or asset sale.

When one company purchases most or all of another company's shares to gain control of that company, it is also termed as an acquisition. Buying more than 50% of a target firm's stock and other assets enable the acquirer to make critical decisions about the acquired assets without seeking the approval of the acquired company's shareholders. The target company either becomes an associate, subsidiary, or part of a subsidiary of the acquirer.

3. Purpose of Any Acquisition

The purpose of acquisition obviously differs from case to case; however, before commencing due diligence or drafting of definitive documents, it is important to brief the professional teams about the exact purpose of acquisition so that they stay focused during the conduct of due diligence or drafting documentation. Described below are some of the key purposes:

  a. **To improve the performance** of the target company: Here, the acquiring company, more often a profit-driven private equity player, is highly involved in the day-to-day activities of the target company. Typical austerity measures like cost reduction are employed. Synonymous with turnaround acquisitions wherein the target company needs a financial or strategic makeover.

  b. **To weed out duplication and redundancy**: Acquirer aims to arrest the financial bleed of duplication, thereby boosting consolidated profits.

  c. **To acquire the know-how**: Certain heavyweights often acquire smaller players with niche value props, say breakthrough technology or novel business model. The common motive is to take the niche to a higher scale and outpace the competition.

d. **To achieve economies of scale**: When a big company acquires several smaller companies, it helps them reduce production costs and boost profitability.

e. **To scout for seed stage prospects:** The acquisition happens at a very early stage of the target's life cycle, to own a disruptive technology or product with the potential to kill competition and create a new market.

f. **To create value:** Acquisition is aimed at improving target company's performance for effecting its sale at a profit.

g. **To consolidate operations**: The motive is elimination of competition from a low demand, high supply market.

h. **To achieve business acceleration:** A smaller company is acquired to help accelerate market access for its products.

i. **To acquire key resources:** Key resources, skills, intellectual property, technologies or market positioning are acquired; often the outcome of a 'build vs. buy' deliberation.

j. **To profit from speculation**: Acquirer aims to cash in on the future growth potential of the acquired set-up.

Whilst on the topic of 'purpose of acquisition' I must share an extremely important and large transaction, where I was representing the founders of a highly-reputed, large, Indian chemical company, and the buyer was an international company. Over familial reasons, they wanted to exit the business as quickly as possible. The objective was conveyed to me in explicit terms: avoid any hard positioning during negotiations. Because of the large consideration, I insisted on doing a vendor due diligence, and the clients fortunately accepted my request. During the due diligence, I found many loose ends which had to be fixed before presenting the data to the purchasers. We worked overnight and cleared as many issues as we could. In all fairness, I prepared a comprehensive list of pending issues and shared it upfront with the purchaser, along with an action plan to resolve them in a time-bound manner. I also assured them of my unconditional support. I consciously did this to avoid any hard negotiations (or reduction in consideration). Since we shared all pending issues upfront with the purchaser and showed our willingness to resolve them, they could not ask for any discount or reduction in the price. On the contrary, they appreciated our transparent way of handling things, and the deal was closed in record time.

4. Legal Due Diligence

In addition to the legal process, I would think due diligence is an extremely important step for any M&A and merits serious consideration by all concerned. It is also in line with the first tenet of the GPS Paradigm of acquiring 'ground intelligence' before conceiving the idea of any M&A in any form in any industry. In the next chapter, I have elaborated the scope and intent of ground intelligence, as I envisage it, under the GPS Paradigm for M&As. Hence, here I will merely touch upon the legal, financial, technical, and environmental due diligence which are equally important from the process point of view.

In my three decades of experience, having worked on a few mega and complex legal due diligence processes for M&As spanning more than six to nine months, in conjunction with national and international teams specializing in tax, technical, and environmental due diligence, I can vouch for the fact that M&A due diligence merits a more **structured, focused and solution-centric team approach. Unfortunately, that is not always the case.**

Whilst any purchaser is entitled to conduct a detailed legal due diligence before any M&A, I think even vendors should engage consultants (legal & tax) to conduct at least a **limited legal due diligence** (also called as a **Vendor DD**), before their data is made available to the purchaser. This precaution should be made a matter of prudent practice as it would help the vendors to take retrospective steps for correcting past violations or compliance, get alerts on critical violations which may be red flags for the purchaser, which may call for additional representation, warranty, and even a stronger indemnity.

Ideally, before commencing drafting of definitive documents, every purchaser or acquirer should conduct thorough legal due diligence, which should include the following:

- Constitutional documents (Memorandum of Association and Articles of Associations or Partnership or LLP Agreement)
- Material contracts or business practices followed in manufacturing, marketing & distribution, research and development
- Secretarial & legal compliance, like board & shareholders' minutes, statutory registers & regulatory filings, licences and approvals
- Employee contracts and HR compliance
- Ownership of assets (tangible and intangible, including intellectual property)
- Borrowings/loan documents
- Litigations by or against the company and promoters

A couple of practical things to be borne in mind whilst conducting due diligence:

- Ensure that all consultants are briefed about the broad objectives of the M&As and JVs, and the core of the business module so that they are aware of the concerns, and are rightly focused
- Get regularly briefed or updated on the findings

- Integrate the inputs from all consultants, including legal, tax, technical, environmental with a tabulated risk matrix, and

- Engage experienced hands for conduct of due diligence. It is seen that occasionally law and audit firms depute extremely junior resources or at times even interns, which is a seriously flawed practice

I was engaged by an international private equity fund desirous of investing substantial money in a Chennai-based IT company. Whilst conducting the due diligence, the senior management of the investee company repeatedly assured us that their operations are absolutely clean, and that they maintain total transparency. However, many of their large customer contracts were not produced, and we were told that they followed the business practice of solely raising invoices. Every officer of the company offered a different explanation for not possessing written customer contracts. I raised this as a serious concern with my clients, who confessed to me that they were aware of the discrepancy but were waiting for a factual confirmation. As a practical solution, I asked the investee team to secure an email confirmation on the terms of contract at least from their key customers, which they refused outright. While the transaction lingered, one fine day, a newspaper report revealed an IT raid on the company as they were booking massive bogus revenue entries. The transaction obviously got aborted.

Having conducted some massive legal due diligence processes, I may add that when the data is enormous, it is advisable to (a) split teams and fix responsibilities, (b) ask them to focus on identifying key issues, (c) hold regular review meetings, (d) freeze the reporting format with clients in advance, and (d) update clients on a weekly basis.

The point I am trying to make here is that legal due diligence is an extremely critical exercise and needs to be handled with utmost thoroughness and precision, especially given the growing complexity of business models.

5. Indian Jurisprudence on Critical M&A Components

As mentioned above, the underlying idea of this book is to share my perspectives on future M&As and JVs, given the mounting technological dominance on economy and environment, as also to highlight the criticality of the GPS Paradigm in pursuing M&As or JVs. I have consciously avoided touching upon the nitty-gritty and the timelines of the legal process involved under any laws for implementing any M&A which is broadly like global norms save for a few local compliance requirements. Suffice to state that M&As begin with a meeting of minds of the decision makers (either directly or via intermediaries like investment bankers or trusted advisors), followed by Board approval, valuation to determine swap ratio, due diligence (legal, financial, technical, environmental & reputational), shareholders' and creditors' meetings (which are court-convened in India), approvals/consent from industry regulators, if any, and from securities regulator (in case of listed entities). Instead, I thought it would be worthwhile to study the jurisprudence around key M&A issues which would help understand the M&A core in the specific context of the GPS Paradigm.

As a corporate lawyer, I take immense pride in appreciating, more than acknowledging, the alacrity and acumen of the Indian jurisprudence in dealing with critical M&A components. Typical M&A challenges like valuation intricacies, protection of employees' rights, public interest, or scheme amendments post sanction have today become more daunting than ever before. It is heartening to note the consistently progressive views of the Indian judiciary on these sticky challenges, both in the High Courts and the Supreme Court of India. It would not be out of place to discuss a select few but remarkably representative court observations and decisions in the specific context of the GPS Paradigm, as several complexities of future M&A deals can be better grasped in the guiding light of these pivotal judgments. The precise and purposeful judgments are self-explanatory; in that they address the crux of the matter, devoid of the overwhelming ambiguity and disorienting diversity of interpretations.

Let us appreciate the essence of a few landmark judgments in their verbatim forms. We begin with a slice of history.

Before 1928, 'amalgamation' was a vague term. A company was allowed to dispose of its undertaking to another company, but it was necessary to invoke the 'winding up' machinery. The arrangement would provide for the voluntary liquidation of the given company, as also the sale of the undertaking and assets by its liquidator to a third company formed for the specific purpose of the said acquisition. The arrangement also directed the purchasing company to undertake and indemnify the liquidators against the liabilities of the two amalgamating companies. **Assets could be transferred by executing several conveyances to which the liquidator was held party. Assignments had to be negotiated, and dissolution could not take place until after the completion of the winding up. To help avoid duty payments on a whole series of transfer deeds, the parliament incorporated the Section 54 provisions in the Companies Act, 1928 (UK)**, which later continued as Sections 391-396 in the Companies Act, 1956 (India) and as Section 230 in the latest Companies Act, 2013 to facilitate corporate amalgamations. Accordingly, particular assets could only be transferred with the consent of some third party, and it was binding on the liquidator of the transferring company to obtain that consent. This was the broad legal framework of 'merger' or 'amalgamation' schemes created to facilitate transfer of divisions or business operations of one company to another.

The Indian company law deals with terms like compromise, arrangement, and reconstruction but defines only the term "arrangement" to include any reorganization of the company share capital, either through consolidation of shares of different classes, division into shares of different classes, or both.

The terms, 'compromise' and 'reconstruction' have not been defined even under the English Companies Act. They may imply any form of internal reorganization of the company or its affairs, as well as schemes for the merger of two or more companies, or for the division of one into two or more companies (now known as demerger).

Compromise implies some element of accommodation on each side. Pennington on Company Law has observed that *"A compromise has been described as an agreement terminating a dispute between parties as to the rights of one or both of them, or modifying the undoubted rights of a party which he has difficulty in enforcing. An arrangement is a wider class of agreement and it need be in no way analogous to a compromise, so that it will include agreements which modify rights about which there is no dispute, and which can be enforced without difficulty."*

In Guardian Assurance Co., reported in (1917) 1 Ch 431, the English Court had refused to sanction a scheme on the ground that there was no dispute or difficulty to be resolved by compromise or arrangement. The Court of Appeal **reversed** the decision, stating that the word "arrangement" should not be limited to something analogous to a compromise. A scheme providing for the holder of the majority of shares to acquire the minority, on favorable terms, is within the scope of the section.

It is pertinent to note that the terms 'compromise', 'arrangement' and 'reconstruction' used in India are of the widest character, ranging from simple compromise to amalgamation of various companies, including complete reorganization of their capital, assets, loans, and the like.

Let us study the judicial style, stance, approach and treatment under broad heads of mission-critical significance for business and industry:

(a) Single Window Clearance

The court process of any scheme of M&A in India requires board approval, an approval from the court-convened general meeting, followed by court sanction after hearing all concerned parties – including shareholders and regulators, as also objections to the scheme, if any. For listed Indian companies, additional approval from the Stock Exchanges governed by the Securities and Exchange Board of India (SEBI) – equivalent to Securities and Exchange Commission in the US (SEC) – is mandatory. Under the new Companies Act, 2013, it is now possible to merge an Indian company into a foreign company as per the exchange control regulations.

As stated above, any M&A scheme is a comprehensive document dealing with asset transfer (tangible and intangible), technology and intellectual property – including brands with goodwill, liabilities (secured and unsecured), licences and regulatory approvals, and employees. The law allows for complete and conclusive flexibility to draw up a scheme facilitating a seamless transfer of business. The courts in India have hence treated such schemes as a **single window approval** for all that is required to effectively transfer the business from one company to another.

The Bombay High Court in the case of PMP Auto Industries reported in 1994 (80) Comp Cases 289 observed that *"Section 391 invests the court with powers to approve or sanction a scheme of amalgamation/ arrangement, which is for the benefit of the company. In doing so, if there are any other things which, for effectuation, require a special procedure to be followed except reduction of capital, then the court has power to sanction them while sanctioning the scheme itself. It would not be necessary for the company to resort to other provisions of the Companies Act or to follow other procedures prescribed for bringing about the changes requisite for effectively implementing the scheme, which is sanctioned by the court. Section 391 is a complete code as held by the courts but, in my view, it is also intended to be in the nature of* **'single window clearance'** *system* **to ensure that the parties are not put to avoidable, unnecessary and cumbersome procedure of making repeated application to the court for various other alterations or changes** *which might be needed effectively to* implement the sanctioned scheme whose overall fairness and feasibility has been judged by the court under Section 394 of the Act."

Further, the court observed: "The introduction of Section 394A, however, has made some change. It is now necessary for the court before sanctioning any amalgamation, to issue notice to the Company Law Board of every application under Section 391 or 394 and to take into consideration the representation, if any, made to it by the Company Law Board before passing any other under either section. I see no reason why the Company Law Board cannot raise all its objections at this stage. The notice under this section appears to be treated as a mere formality. If the Company Law Board has any objection to the proposed scheme of amalgamation, they must come forward and state them while opposing the scheme of amalgamation. It would then be possible for the court to appreciate the objections, if any, and adjudicate thereupon. If the court is satisfied that the objection based on the alteration of the memorandum has no substance, the court itself can decide it then and there and sanction the scheme even if it means a consequential amendment of the memorandum of association."

(b) Consent of Members/Creditors/Class

The scheme must be approved by the members (including any class) or creditors (including any class) as the case may be, depending upon the nature of the scheme. Such meeting is held on the directions of the court. In doing so, the court does not decide what classes of members or creditors should be made parties to the scheme. It is the company's prerogative to decide in accordance with what the scheme purports to achieve. **For example, if rights of ordinary shareholders are to be altered, but those of preference shareholders are to be excluded, a meeting of ordinary shareholders will be necessary but not of preference shareholders.** If there are different groups within a class whose interests are different from the rest of the class, or which are to be treated differently under the scheme, such groups must be treated as separate classes for the purpose of the scheme.

Great care must be taken while considering what constitutes a class for the purpose of the scheme. If meetings of the proper class have not been held, the court may not sanction the scheme. The English Court in the case of Sovereign Life Assurance Co. V. Dodd (1892) 2 QB 573, held: **"In order to constitute a class, members belonging to the class must form a homogeneous group with commonality of interest. If people with heterogeneous interests are combined in a class, naturally, the majority having common interest may ride roughshod over the minority representing a distinct interest."**

The Gujarat High Court in the case of *Maneckchowk and Ahmedabad Mfg. Co. Ltd 1970 (49) Company Cases 819* observed that *"counsel for the applicants relied on the commentary by Buckley on the Companies Act 13th Edition Page 406, wherein it has been set out that the creditors composing different classes must have different interests. The test laid down was could the different state of facts existing among different creditors affect their minds and their judgment. In such a situation they could constitute a separate class by themselves. Another test was that member belonging to the class must form a homogeneous group with commonality of interest. The next test would be is whether the nature of compromise offered to different group of classes are different. If a different compromise is offered to different creditors those would constitute a class by themselves. It was set out that the group styled as a class should ordinarily be homogeneous and must have commonality of interest and the compromise offered to them must be identical."*

(c) Scrutiny of the Scheme

An oft-raised question which bothers companies and concerned parties is: How would the court examine a scheme? This question has been answered in a very eloquent manner by the Gujarat High Court in the case of Navjivan Mills Co. Ltd., 42 Company Cases 265, wherein the court has observed in Page 320 that:

"The scheme should not be examined in the way a 'carping critic', a 'hair splitting expert', a 'meticulous accountant' or a 'fastidious

counsel' would do it. It must be tested from the point of view of an ordinary reasonable shareholder acting in a business-like manner taking with his comprehension and bearing in mind all the circumstances prevailing at the time when the meeting was called upon to consider the scheme in question. It has to ascertain that the majority vote was honestly obtained, that the majority acted honestly, that no financial or arithmetic jugglery was perpetuated either upon the creditors or shareholders."

(d) Potential Flaws in the Scheme

The Chancery Division of the English Court in the case of Sussex Brick Co. Ltd., reported in [1960] 30 Comp. Cases 536 whilst accepting the likelihood of this situation has astutely clarified as follows:

"Although it might be possible to find faults in a scheme, that would not be sufficient ground to reject it. Scheme must be obviously unfair, patently unfair, unfair to the meanest intelligence. It cannot be said that no scheme can be effective to bind a dissenting shareholder unless it complies to the extent of 100 per cent. **It is the consistent view of the courts that no scheme can be said to be foolproof and it is possible to find faults in a particular scheme but that by itself is not enough to warrant a dismissal of the petition for sanction of the scheme.** The courts have gone further to say that a scheme must be held to be unfair to the meanest intelligence before it can be rejected. It must be affirmatively proved to the satisfaction of the court that the scheme is unfair before the scheme can be rejected by the court."

(e) Broad Parameters Adopted by Courts in India for Examining the Scheme

The Supreme Court of India in its leading judgment in the case of *Miheer H. Mafatlal v. Mafatlal Industries Limited 1996 (87) Company Cases 792* has put forth a very interesting observation on page 813:

The Supreme Court observed that "*Section 394 casts an obligation on the court to be satisfied that the scheme for amalgamation or merger was not contrary to public interest. The basic principle of such satisfaction is none other than the broad and general principles inherent in any compromise or settlement entered into between parties that it should not be unfair or contrary to public policy or unconscionable. In amalgamation of companies, the courts have evolved the principle of 'prudent business management test' or that the scheme should not be a device to evade law."*

The Supreme Court, in Mihir Mafatlal's case, aptly observed that the scope and ambit of the jurisdiction of the company court is clearly and unambiguously earmarked. Following are the crystal-clear contours of such jurisdiction with reference to Section 391 of the Companies Act, 1956, and which hold true even under the Companies Act of 2013:

1. *The sanctioning* **court has to see to it that all the requisite statutory procedure for supporting such a scheme has been complied** *with and that the requisite meetings as contemplated by Section 391(1)(a) have been held.*

2. *That the scheme put up for sanction of the court is backed up by the requisite majority vote as required by Section 391(2).*

3. *That the concerned meetings of the creditors or members or any class of them had the relevant material to enable the voters to arrive at an informed decision for approving the scheme in question. That the majority decision of the concerned class of voters is just and fair to the class as a whole so as to legitimately bind even the dissenting members of that class.*

4. *That all necessary material indicated by Section 393(1)(a) is placed before the voters at the concerned meetings as contemplated by Section 391(1).*

5. *That all the requisite material contemplated by the proviso to sub-section 391(2) is placed before the court by the concerned applicant seeking sanction for such a scheme and the court gets satisfied about the same.*

6. *That the proposed scheme of compromise and arrangement is not found to be violative of any provision of law and is not contrary to public policy. For ascertaining the real purpose underlying the scheme with a view to be satisfied on this aspect, the court, if necessary, can pierce the veil of apparent corporate purpose underlying the scheme and can judiciously x-ray the same.*

7. *That the company court has also to satisfy itself that members or class of members or creditors or class of creditors were acting bonafide and in good faith and were not coercing the minority in order to promote and interest adverse to that of the latter comprising the same class whom they purported to represent.*

8. *That the scheme as a whole is also found to be just, fair and reasonable from the point of view of prudent men of business taking a commercial decision beneficial to the class represented by them for whom the scheme is meant.*

9. *Once the aforesaid broad parameters about the requirements of a scheme for getting sanction of the court are found to have been met,* ***the court will have no further jurisdiction to sit in appeal over the commercial wisdom of the majority of the class of persons who with their open eyes have given their approval to the scheme even if in the view of the court there could be a better scheme for the company and its members or creditors for whom the scheme is framed.*** *The court cannot refuse to sanction such a scheme on that ground as it would otherwise amount to the court exercising appellate jurisdiction over the scheme rather than its supervisory jurisdiction.*

(f) Minute Scrutiny and Independent Conclusion

The Supreme Court in its leading judgment in the case of *Miheer H. Mafatlal v. Mafatlal Industries Limited 1996 (87) Company Cases 792* made a highly metaphorical and enlightening observation on page 813: "However, the further question remains whether the court has jurisdiction like an appellate authority to minutely scrutinize the scheme and to arrive at an independent conclusion whether the scheme should be permitted to go through or not when the majority of the creditors or members or their respective classes have approved the scheme as required by Section 391(2). On this aspect the nature of compromise or arrangement between the company and the creditors and members has to be kept in view.

It is the commercial wisdom of the parties to the scheme, who have taken an informed decision about the usefulness and propriety of the scheme, by supporting it by the requisite majority vote and that has to be kept in view by the court. **The court certainly would not act as a court of appeal and sit in judgment over the informed view of the concerned parties to the compromise as the same would be in the realm of corporate and commercial wisdom of the concerned parties. The court has neither the expertise nor the jurisdiction to delve deep into the commercial wisdom exercised by the creditors and members of the company who have ratified the scheme by requisite majority. Consequently, the company court's jurisdiction to that extent is peripheral and supervisory and not appellate. The court acts like an umpire in a game of cricket who has to see that both the teams play their game according to the rules and do not overstep the limits. But subject to that how best the game is to be played is left to the players and not to the umpire."**

(g) Mathematical Precision of Valuations

Literally every scheme of any M&A is challenged on the valuation on the pretext that (i) the valuation is loaded in favour of one company versus the other, or (ii) the methodology adopted is wrong and hence the valuation is incorrect.

In a landmark decision of the Supreme Court in the merger of TOMCO with HLL reported in (1994) 4 Company LJ 267 (para 3) the court made a historic observation on any valuation, namely: *"The jurisdiction of the court in sanctioning any merger is not to ascertain with mathematical accuracy whether the valuation satisfies the arithmetical test. A company* court does not exercise an appellate jurisdiction. It is not required to interfere only because the figure arrived at by the valuer was not as good as it would have been if another method would have been adopted. What is imperative is that such determination should not have been contrary to law and that it was not unfair for the shareholders of the company, which was being merged. The court's obligation is to be satisfied that valuation was in accordance with law and it was carried out by an independent body." The court went on to further observe:

"...certainly, it is not part of the judicial process to examine entrepreneurial activities to ferret out flaws. The court is least equipped for such oversights. Nor indeed is it a function of the judges in our constitutional scheme. We do not think that the internal management, business activity or institutional operation of public bodies can be subjected to inspection by the court. To do so, is incompetent and improper and, therefore, out of bounds."

In fact, earlier, the Bombay High Court in the case of Piramal Spinning and Weaving Mills Ltd. observed that *"the valuation of shares is a technical matter which requires considerable skill and expertise. There is bound to be difference of opinion as to what the correct value of the share of any given company is. Simply because it is possible to value the shares in a manner different from the one which has been adopted in a given case, it cannot be said that the valuation which has been agreed upon is unfair. Unless the person who challenges the valuation arrived at is grossly unfair, the court will not disturb the scheme of amalgamation, which has been approved by the shareholders of the two companies.*

Valuation is ultimately a matter of expert's opinion. If there is more than one method of valuation, a valuation would vary if different methods were adopted. Shares are the property of shareholders and they are ultimate and the best judges of the value which they would put on their shares. The question of valuation is obviously one about which opinions may differ. It is possible in such cases to criticize figures, offers and balance sheets, and argue about matters of fairness and unfairness. The test of fairness is whether the offer is fair to the offeree as a body and not whether it is fair to a particular shareholder in a peculiar circumstance of his own case."

(h) **Employee Protection**

In an era of rampant unrest, mass upheavals, and massive discontentment rooted in perpetual economic downturns, protection of employee rights is a herculean task, more so given the fact that it is often deemed to be contrary to the very objectives that the JV pursues. The court has shared insightful observations on this crucial matter in several cases.

The Supreme Court, in the case of TOMCO merger with HLL mentioned above, was faced with the objection raised by the employees that the merger will cause unemployment or that it may result in many employees of the TOMCO being rendered surplus. The Supreme Court observed that a *"scheme of amalgamation cannot be faulted on apprehension and speculation as to what might possibly happen in future. Improved technology and scientific method result in better employment prospects. Anxiety should be to protect workers and not to obstruct development and growth.* ***Maybe that advanced technology may reduce the manpower, but so long as those who are working are protected, they are not entitled to hinder in modernisation or merger under misapprehension that future employment of the same number of workers may stand curtailed."***

In an earlier judgment the **Gujarat High Court in the case of Navjivan Mills Co.** Ltd., reported in (1972) 42 Comp Cases 265 had observed that *"if the scheme is primarily directed to inject health into a sick industrial company, the court should examine the scheme from an additional angle, namely, what is the role of such an undertaking in the economic and industrial life of this country."* The court further observed that rather than allowing the company to be wound up, meaning thereby that it should reach a civil death, throwing workers out of their employment by putting an end to the existence of the company, serious endeavours and sacrifices be made by all concerned such as by shareholders and creditors in order to ensure that the industrial undertaking can be rejuvenated and restarted. The court observed that in the present state of our society, a victim of vicious phenomena of rising prices and depleting employment, the court cannot remain oblivious to this aspect.

(i) M&As Against Public Interest

A question is always raised from various quarters about protecting public interest. Objection was raised to the TOMCO merger with HLL that the merger is against public interest. It was supported by relying on the terms of agreement wherein it was mentioned that immovable assets worth Rs. 800 crores were being transferred to a subsidiary of foreign company for Rs. 30 crores only. Secondly, as a result of the merger, Unilever PLC, whose shareholding was being reduced from 51% to 40%, was also given additional shares through preferential allotment in order to maintain its 51% holding. It was further argued that there were only two competing companies manufacturing soap and detergents. With the merger, there would be no competition and that it would result in creating virtual monopoly in favour of HL, which could result not only in deterioration of quality, but also escalation of price.

The Supreme Court after hearing all parties stated that Section 11 of the Foreign Exchange Regulation Act, 1973 (FERA – the then Indian Exchange Control Regulations), which empowered the Reserve Bank of India (RBI – the Central bank regulating foreign exchange) to put restrictions on transfer of any asset in India to person resident outside India, has been repealed in 1993. The FERA has been amended specifically to encourage foreign participation in business in India. The bar of having more than 40% shares in an Indian company by non-residents has been lifted. Secondly, in order to give greater freedom to the companies for doing business in India, the Monopolies and Restrictive Trade Practices Act, 1969 (MRTP Act) has been amended. No prior approval of the Government is necessary for amalgamation of companies any more under the MRTP Act. Considering these statutory changes, the Supreme Court observed that just because 51% of the shares are being given to foreign company, the scheme cannot be said to be against public policy. The MRTP Act has now been repealed and is replaced by the Competition Act, 2002 which gives a lot of autonomy in this regard.

The Supreme Court also observed in Para 5 that *"the concept of 'public interest' cannot be put in a straightjacket. It is a dynamic concept which keeps on changing. It has been explained in Black's Law Dictionary as something in which the public, the community at large, has some pecuniary interest, or some interest by which their legal rights or liabilities are affected. It does not mean anything so narrow as mere curiosity, whereas the interest of the particular locality which may be affected by the matters in question. Interest shared by citizens generally in affairs of local, State or national government."*

It is an expression of wide amplitude. It may have different connotation and understanding when used in service law and yet a different meaning in criminal law than civil law, and its shade may be entirely different in company law. But when it is with subsidiary of foreign company, the consideration may be entirely different. It is not the interest of shareholders or the employees only, but the interest of society which may have to be examined. And a scheme valid and good may yet be bad if it is against public interest.

Section 394 casts an obligation on the court to be satisfied that the scheme of amalgamation or merger was not contrary to public interest. The basic principle of such satisfaction is none other than the broad and general principles inherent in any compromise or settlement entered between parties that it should not be unfair or contrary to public policy or unconscionable. **In amalgamation of companies the courts have evolved the principle of 'prudent business management test' or that the scheme should not be a device to evade law.** *But when the court is concerned with a scheme of merger with a subsidiary of a foreign company, then the test is not only whether the scheme shall result in maximizing profits of the shareholders,* or whether the interest of employees was protected, but it has to ensure that the merger shall not result in impeding promotion of industry or obstruct growth of national economy. Liberalized economic policy is to achieve this goal."

Further, at para 77 the court observed that *"nor do we think that 'public interest', which is to be taken into account as an element against approval of amalgamation, would include a mere future possibility of merger resulting in a situation where the interests of the consumer might be adversely affected. If, however, in future, the working of the company turns out to be against the interest of the consumers or the employees, suitable corrective steps may be taken by appropriate authorities in accordance with law. As has been said in the case of Fertilizer Corporation Kamgar Union (1981) 2SCR 52 page 77: '... It is not part of the judicial process to examine entrepreneurial activities to ferret out flaws. The court is least equipped for such oversights. Nor indeed is it the function of the judges in our constitutional scheme."*

(j) Scheme Amendments Post Court-Sanction

This is a million-dollar question which bothers every stakeholder during the preparatory stage of the M&A. I am pleased to mention here that the M&A which I was handling for Duphar-Interfran Ltd. (an affiliate of Solvay Pharmaceuticals), the Bombay High Court reported in (2002) SEBI & Corporate Laws Vol 35 page 579 relying on the earlier landmark decision of the Supreme Court the following:

"Section 392 of the Act gives wide power to the company court to make addition to the scheme or omission therefrom solely for the purpose of making it workable. In fact, in S.K. Gupta v. K.P. Jain AIR 1979 SC 734, the Supreme Court went so far to say that, strictly speaking, omission of the original sponsor and substituting another one would not change the basic fabric of the scheme. The Supreme Court in S. K. Gupta's case quoted with approval the observation of the Gujarat High Court in Mansukhlal v. M. V. Shah (1976) 46 Com. Cases 279 as:

'The frames of the company law in India have conferred statutory powers on the High Court to make such modification in the compromise or arrangement as the court may consider necessary for the proper working of the compromise and arrangement. The power of the widest amplitude has been conferred on the court under Section 392(1)(b), and the width and magnitude of the power can be gauged from the language employed in Section 392(1)(a) which confers a sort of a supervisory role on the court during the period the scheme of compromise or arrangement is being implemented. Reading Clauses (a) and (b) of Section 392(1) it appears that Parliament did not want the court to be functus officio as soon as the scheme of compromise and arrangement is sanctioned by it. The court has a continuing supervision over the implementation of compromise and arrangement. **Unenvisaged, unanticipated, unforeseen or even unimaginable hitches, obstruction, and impediments may arise in the course of implementation of a scheme of compromise and arrangement, and if on every such occasion sponsors have to go back to the parties concerned for seeking their approval for a modification and then seek the approval of the court, it would be a long drawn out, protracted, time-consuming process, with no guarantee of result and the whole scheme of compromise and arrangement may be mutilated in the process.** Parliament has, therefore thought it fit to trust the wisdom of the court rather than go back to the interested parties. If the parties have several times to decide the modification with the democratic process, the good part of an election machinery apart, the dirt may step in, the conflicting interest may be bought and sold, and, in the process the whole scheme of compromise and arrangement may be jettisoned. **In order, therefore, to guard against this eventuality and situation, which is clearly envisageable, Parliament has conferred power on the court, not only to make modifications event at the time of sanctioning the scheme, but at any time thereafter during the period the scheme is being implemented.** Conceding that before the court sanctions the scheme, it partakes the character of an emerging contract between the company and the creditors and members; once the court approves it, it becomes a statutorily enforceable contract even on *dissidents, with power in the court to modify, amend, or to correct or revise the contract – the outer periphery or the limit on the power being that, after testing it on the anvil of probabilities, surrounding circumstances and the prevalent state of affairs, it can be done for the proper working of the compromise and arrangement, and subject to this limit on the court's power, the power seems to be absolute and of the widest amplitude, and it would be unwise to curtail it by the process of interpretation."*

Chapter 3

Institutionalizing M&A Capabilities: Need of the Hour

Notwithstanding the diversity of causes and circumstances from company to company, any M&A deal is essentially a **business process** governed by generally accepted principles of prudence and precision, as also industry best practices. At the same time, M&A is essentially a **strategic decision** calling for a comprehensive study of the industry and market environment, including the motives, motivations, challenges and opportunities for growth, and measurable value creation. Being proactive is critical to M&As as it would be unwise to react only in the event of compulsion. Instead, M&A-related study should be treated as an ongoing exercise to evaluate potential targets or acquirers, as the case may be. A detailed analysis of competitive edge and valuation multiples is a given to help identify one's stature in the given sector, as also foresee the probable footprints on the M&A horizon – whether applicable to potential acquirers or likely targets.

In today's competitive world, every enterprise – looking to thrive or trying to survive, big fish or greenhorn, conglomerate or family-owned, global or local – would do well to look back and learn from the towering M&A precedents that have left an indelible mark in global corporate history. The ease of banking finance, supportive capital markets, and abundant cash flows have together fueled M&A activity like never before in recent years. More importantly, the need and significance of M&A is itself bursting at the seams of infinite possibilities. Among other things, an unprecedented surge in the number of SMEs, MSMEs, and start-ups has triggered this evolution in the wake of:

- Phenomenal business disruption, thanks to the fast-paced technological innovation
- Continual product and process innovation in line with evolving market needs
- Marked rise in the entrepreneurial mindset due to value-added education, competition, and globalization
- COVID-19-induced job losses, rampant business slowdowns and imminent shutdowns

M&A will become a key 'business tool', nay a 'standard protocol' as much to thrive as to survive. It is a foregone conclusion that modern-day entrepreneurs will have to grasp the basic contours of M&As if they are to reimagine and re-engineer businesses to keep pace with the evolving paradigms of tomorrow.

The entrepreneurial fraternity – comprising both veterans and novices – would now need to think M&As for the sake of survival ahead of growth and sustainability. Going forward, the diversity of, and innovation in, M&A models would spell the difference between leaders and followers. The need to recognize **M&A as a key business process** is clear and evident from the following analysis based on historical pointers; statistical findings and expert opinion; insightful case studies; M&A strategy formulation and execution principles; and prominent exemplars of 'M&A as a strategy'.

Historical pointers

Given the phenomenal rise of economic liberalization, privatization and globalization over the years, companies across different verticals and spheres have had to make fundamental changes to their ways of doing business. The reason is obvious: to develop, enhance and retain their competitive edge, as also thrive in what is clearly an ever-evolving, ever-demanding consumer landscape.

Notwithstanding the potency of the usual growth strategies – whether aggressive marketing, focused research, or disruptive innovation – the global business village of today calls for a more effective and sustainable way of accelerating profits and potential: the inorganic route of M&A transactions.

As we have seen in an earlier section, the first decade of the century established M&A as an integral part of a successful growth strategy. Many companies delivered superior shareholder returns, soaring high on the wings of M&A, which invariably creates value if built upon a replicable and scrupulous model.[1] Thanks to the ubiquity of high-value deals amounting to millions of dollars, it was not long before M&As became an accepted business strategy on a globalized scale.[2]

1. Implementation of M&A as a Business Strategy

1.1 M&A as Internal Department in a Company

In my three decades of experience as an M&A lawyer, I have found that only MNCs and large, family-owned companies engage structured and focused M&A teams, which is precisely why they are able to seamlessly develop and implement their growth strategies. I have seen mid-sized companies place their faith in external trusted advisors, whereas small and medium companies hire external consultants on need basis. Start-ups are a whole new happening breed, discernibly more open to striking offbeat, unheard of M&As and JVs across the unlikeliest of sectors and spheres. The start-up world, as I see it, is fast evolving as they are naturally attuned to the GPS Paradigm. This phenomenon is evident from the

---

1   http://www.aaronrichards.com/m-a-strategy.html
2   https://www.hindustantimes.com/business/the-inevitable-logic-of-m-as/story-eeL9KgPwVvlyJV8ljIqIbN.html

speed at which unicorns are born. However, I have found them singularly focused on technological innovation. They also need to develop technical capabilities and incisive depth to manage M&As and JVs.

There are various sources that stress on the creation of an internal department for M&A to bolster its growth strategy. Given the global impact of M&A transactions, they remain a critical tool for growth and long-term shareholder value creation, reaping benefits such as building scale and performance improvements. Building internal M&A capabilities should hence be a key focus area of every corporate. The executive team would act as a steward to help determine if a specific deal would fit into a company's growth plan, make the transactional process disciplined by assembling the right people, and come up with strategic alternatives in case of a setback.[3]

It has been firmly established that the internal organization managing a company's M&A processes is a major contributor to the success of its deals.[4] Creation of a dedicated M&A team is considered best practice since it manages and optimizes all critical variables. [5] Professionalization of the M&A process is a standard that holds true for all transactions.[6] A dedicated M&A team is absolutely necessary to ensure adequate planning, to provide an integration plan, as also to identify and eliminate redundancies in a company's workforce.[7]

Further, an institutionalized M&A team manages due diligence, both financial and legal, for establishing potential deal value. It can provide a strategic outlook on due diligence to help ascertain

---

3 https://www2.deloitte.com/content/dam/Deloitte/us/Documents/mergers-acqisitions/us-ma-making-the-deal-work-strategy.pdf
4 https://www.mckinsey.com/business-functions/strategy-and-corporate-finance/our-insights/building-the-right-organization-for-mergers-and-acquisitions#
5 https://www.smartsheet.com/content/merger-acquisition-strategies
6 https://mkt-bcg-com-public-images.s3.amazonaws.com/public-pdfs/legacy-documents/file15069.pdf
7 https://blog.careerminds.com/mergers-and-acquisitions-deal-team

if the potential deal value is realistic and commercially attractive,[8] contributing to transformational development.[9] An internal M&A team fuels cost-cutting practices and ensures agile and focused deal making.[10]

In the context of the post-merger integration process, an internal team ensures time-saving efficiencies through the use of methodologies, templates, and tools from past integration. Additionally, they possess invaluable knowledge about the company's working approach.[11]

1.2 Characteristics to be Adopted by an M&A Team

Towards maximizing a company's growth strategy, the ideal team must not only be skilled at screening acquisition targets, conducting due diligence, and integrating acquired businesses, but also must have the size, structure, and credibility to influence the rest of the company.[12] **The internal M&A team must possess a clearly defined strategy supporting the company's deal making objectives such as establishing a screening process for deals, having an appropriate breadth of skills with well-defined roles, expertise in key areas, defining leadership as per the strategic goals of the project, working in tandem with other units of the company, namely the business units, R&D and strategy group.**[13] More than the team's size, the collective experience and project-driven approach are more critical to the deal's success, provided the essentials of M&A governance and execution are in place. Such teams are particularly advantageous to industries like utility or broad software, which lack a highly formalized M&A process.[14]

---

8   https://www.strategy-business.com/article/enews092806?gko=2e820
9   https://www.victanis.com/mergers-and-acquisitions-business-strategy
10 http://www.performapartners.com/en/highlights/68-a-shopping-team-to-call-your
11 https://imaa-institute.org/the-role-of-finance-in-successful-serial-ma/
12 *Supra* at 15.
13 Id.
14 https://www.mckinsey.com/business-functions/strategy-and-corporate-finance/our-insights/m-and-38a-teams-when-small-is-beautiful#

The basic corporate tool for effecting a successful M&A is a relatively standardized discounted-cash-flow analysis to identify key elements (including intrinsic and synergy value), due-diligence checklists, and integration team charters.[15] Critical factors include a tight link between corporate strategy and M&A group to decide whether the deal suits the scope, as also to ensure the following: an explicit decision-making process (committee based or standard investment decision process), involvement of functional experts with credible deal experience, facilitating early integration planning for due diligence and learning from prior deals through a formal educational process like post deal workshops and updated playbooks.[16]

Other strategies for ensuring a seamless deal process include establishing a cross-functional team for effecting M&A-related communication among HR, finance, sales, procurement, and other departments.[17] The company must comprehend the industry's value-creation opportunities and challenges, identify and prioritize potential targets and predators, and rigorously plan the post-merger integration process to ensure extraction of optimum deal value.[18]

A dedicated M&A team must have an experienced leader at the helm, helped by competent accountants, investment bankers, and tax attorneys for valuation, due diligence and arriving at a fair deal value. A legal counsel is ideally an experienced business lawyer (preferably trusted advisor) who can structure the transaction, prepare fool-proof documentation, and help judge the deal's compliance with various aspects of the law. HR experts are vital for figuring out logistics such as organizational culture, impact of lay-offs, and training of employees.[19] Companies must also adopt a strategic approach to due diligence

---

15 Id.
16 Id.
17 *Supra* at 16.
18 *Supra* at 17.
19 *Supra* at 18.

(financial, legal, technical, environmental, and reputational), for testing the deal's projected synergies, risk management and key value drivers.[20]

1.3 Theses/Case Studies on M&A as a Business Strategy

The M&A impact on promising markets, in helping companies diversify their portfolios and avail of new opportunities, was duly measured based on a data, time series and association analysis. It was found that M&As are helping companies secure tech capabilities to seek "growth" and "innovation", thereby enabling breakthroughs into the sunrise industry and technology areas. A dissection of the purpose and types of M&A transactions found them a good stepping-stone to explore new sustainability avenues and growth engines.[21]

M&A was identified as an established growth and business strategy. Hailed as a "worldwide phenomenon", M&As were found to be increasingly used for achieving a larger asset base, entering new markets, generating greater market share and additional manufacturing capacities, gaining complementary strengths and competencies, and building a competitive edge in the marketplace.

M&A emergence was also found to one of the most effective methods of corporate structuring, and an integral part of long-term business strategy, pointing out the fact that almost 85% of Indian companies are using M&A as a core growth strategy. M&As were called as 'expression of strategic concepts', very crucial for any country's economy as the engines of growth.[22]

Studying various strategies of business leaders to further performance, M&A was found to be a key process for business growth, showing a

---

20 *Supra* at 19.
21 https://www.mdpi.com/2071-1050/12/1/139/pdf
22 https://www.innovativejournal.in/index.php/ijbm/article/view/389/374

rising trend of M&A activity worldwide to develop new markets or seek transfer of technology and innovation to keep pace with globalization.[23]

Examining the benefits of M&A as a corporate growth strategy, it was stated that they accrue to the shareholders of both acquiring company and acquired company. The manifold benefits include revenue boost, marketing gains, cost reduction for the collective, complementary resources, tax benefits and lower cost for capital.[24]

1.4 Successful Examples of Companies Adopting M&A as a Business Strategy

a. **Disney** has emerged as a strong proponent of M&A by acquiring Pixar, Marvel, Lucasfilm, and 20th Century Fox. With the Pixar acquisition alone, Disney brought more movies to its target audience and boosted its animation practices. Disney's M&A strategy serves as a prime example of a conscious use of M&A to breed more success.[25]

b. **Google** has successfully employed M&A, both to make new market breakthroughs as also to acquire new technology, by acquiring entities such as YouTube, Android and FitBit. Overall, while Google's strategy is definitively focused on strong strategic fits, it is not averse to taking calculated risks.[26]

c. **IBM** developed and executed a strategic and synergistic plan for moving into higher-value software and services. Key themes included business analytics, Smarter Planet, and cloud computing. Consequently, IBM's average acquisition (2002-

---

23 https://scholarworks.waldenu.edu/cgi/viewcontent.cgi?article=9185&context=dissertations
24 https://bib.irb.hr/datoteka/566380.final_paper-ma_activities_as_a_growth_strategy__the_case_of_croatia.pdf
25 https://dealroom.net/blog/mergers-and-acquisitions-as-a-business-growth-strategy
26 Id.

2005) doubled its direct revenue within two years. By 2010, in a paradigm shift, IBM began to be better known for its business analytics capability rather than its computing devices and it surpassed its original financial targets. [27]

d. Since the 1960s, **Cintas** boosted its organic growth through small acquisitions. In the 1990s to 2000, the company spent $3 billion on more than 250 deals, accounting for 40% of its revenue growth. Consequently, sales rose by 20% annually and market capitalization grew by 23% per year to $8.5 billion. Thanks to the smart acquisitions, shareholders reaped an average annual return of almost 21%—five percentage points more than the company's cost of equity. Clearly, the acquisition spree through sectoral highs and lows created significant long-term shareholder value.[28]

2. Competition and Valuation in Tech-Centric M&A Deals

Given the increasing complexity of any business structure due to multiple layers of business combinations and heavy reliance on tech-driven platforms, it would be necessary for the regulators and mainstream M&A consultants to come up with sophisticated methodologies to evaluate and adjudicate issues in the context of competition laws and valuation exercises in tech-centric M&As.

2.1 Competition Law

Generally, competition law watchdogs find it difficult to assess the data privacy and protection challenges of technology-centric M&As. The effect of M&As on data quality is not fully comprehended for a variety of reasons. The purview of consumer welfare has yet to convincingly accommodate the tech issues of consumer data preferences, personal data protection, data innovation, platform switching costs, and the

---

27 *Supra* at 7.
28 https://hbr.org/2003/03/your-best-ma-strategy

restrictive practices of dominant platforms. The law urgently needs to adapt to the peculiarities of the global digital universe. It is pertinent to examine a couple of representative case studies that highlight the exclusivity of tech M&As.

- **Grab-Uber Acquisition**

    In 2018, the Singapore-based ride-hailing company bought the entire Southeast Asian operations and assets of Uber. The latter was granted a 27.5 per cent share in Grab and its chief executive officer was inducted into the board. Competition agencies of the concerned countries were not informed either because mandatory notification thresholds did not apply, or no merger notification was supposedly required by law. Look at the conundrum the deal caused due to the different positions taken by different Southeast Asian nations:

    Indonesia held the deal was not a merger, an asset acquisition without any transfer of control to Grab Indonesia. The **Malaysia** Competition Commission in conjunction with Land Public Transport Commission closely monitored Grab operations post the deal, to check whether the competition was affected in any manner. **Singapore's** Competition and Consumer Commission initiated an investigation as a self-assessment was required by law to decide whether notification is necessary. It was found that the transaction substantially impacted the ride-hailing market in Singapore. Consequently, the Commission imposed many restrictions and penalties on Grab and Uber. **Vietnam** held that Grab got control of more than 50 percent of the market post-acquisition and directed the Competition and Consumer protection department of the Ministry of Industry and Trade to conduct further investigation.

- **Amazon's Dominant Quasi-Monopoly Platform**

    Germany's Federal Cartel Office and the European Commission initiated an investigation of Amazon's treatment meted out to third-party retailers to check whether it used seller data to boost its direct sales. Amazon is the largest online retailer, as also a marketplace in Germany. This dual role can potentially disadvantage rival sellers who are part of the Amazon platform. If the unfair dominance is proved, it will be the first instance of an online marketplace services having been recognized as a market by a competition authority, thereby setting a precedent in other similar cases.

2.2 Valuation Models and GPS Paradigm

Valuation is the basis on which any M&A or JV deal is either structured or shelved. Any valuation is expected to be 'fair', as a rule, not exception. However, what is 'fair' for the seller may not be fair to the buyer. Before delving into the technicalities, I would like to cite an interesting case of an M&A between two public companies that I was handling. A senior partner of a reputed accounting firm was making a detailed presentation on the valuation of both the companies based on accepted methodologies. During the lunch hour, the CFO of the buyer firm asked me about my thoughts on valuation and the swap ratio. In response, I asked him about the average share price of both companies on the stock market during the preceding four months and two weeks. Noting the fluctuations, I asked for historical values of the share price and made my guesstimate based on the statistics shared with me. Post lunch, when the valuer made his recommendation, it exactly matched with my guess. This is not to undermine the scientific methodology of valuation but only to reinforce the fact that valuation is, in the final analysis, a market assessment.

Despite strictly following accepted valuation methodologies, it is possible that post the M&A, the same value may appear exponentially high in the hands of the buyer. Valuation at the end of the day is an 'opinion', albeit there are many scientific and accepted methods to determine valuation, whether Discounted Cash Flow (DCF) based, market value based, asset based, ROI based, or earnings multiples based.

I deeply value the candid submission by our Supreme Court in the landmark decision on the merger of TOMCO with HLL reported in (1994) 4 Company LJ 267 (para 3). The court made a historic observation on any valuation, namely: *"What is imperative is that such determination should not have been contrary to law and that it was not unfair for the shareholders of the company, which was being merged. The court's obligation is to be satisfied that valuation was in accordance with law and it was carried out by an independent body."* The court went on to observe: *"... certainly, it is not part of the judicial process to examine entrepreneurial activities to ferret out flaws. The court is least equipped for such oversights. Nor indeed is it a function of the judges in our constitutional scheme. We do not think that the internal management, business activity or institutional operation of public bodies can be subjected to inspection by the court. To do so, is incompetent and improper and, therefore, out of bounds."*

We must all congratulate the court for being so crystal clear about the process of valuation. I think, given this prudent observation, we must accept that valuation for M&As can be 'fair', not 'perfect'.

In tech valuation, the long-term prospects take precedence over past performance, but there is no single valuation method in vogue due to the extreme volatility and evolving nature of the tech landscape. The key valuation factors for technology businesses include number of subscribers, customer retention, and the strength of frameworks, platforms, and patents. A closer look at the valuation of key deals will help grasp the peculiarities of tech valuation:

    a. **Amazon's** 2009 acquisition of online shoe retailer Zappos was priced at $1.2 billion[29]. The valuation methods used in

---

[29] http://pdf.secdatabase.com/880/0001193125-09-153130.pdf

the deal were a comparable company analysis of players like Blue Nile and Digital River, besides DCF projections of 10-year financials. A precedent transaction analysis looked at eBay and Time Warner deals. Amazon's trading multiples and stock price projections were also considered. Thus, multiple methods were employed to help arrive at a suitable purchase price.

b. **Dell's** acquisition of virtualization player EMC was valued at $67 billion[30], via a blend of cash and common stock. Deal advisor Deloitte prescribed a value prioritization framework to spot most critical areas. 20% of the prioritized opportunities represented 80% of the accretive value, highlighting the criticality of a detailed valuation plan.

c. Electronic manufacturer **BenQ's** acquisition of the Siemens mobile handset business is a sterling example of flawed valuation. Siemen's market multiples were analyzed in conjunction with the DCF method. The acquisition lasted merely one year, given the inherent risks of resource integration that were overlooked by projected cash flows, apart from other factors like culture conflicts.

In valuation methods employed for high-profile tech acquisitions, **ground intelligence** is of utmost importance. Since inaccurate revenue or trading multiples can jeopardize the deal, exhaustive due diligence is a must to arrive at a company's fair value. Accuracy and actionability of core data are thus a critical factor, as also the use of AI and other analytic tools to make accurate projections and extent of strategic fits.

In phases of economic downturn, valuations can help companies gravitate towards striking **unconventional partnerships** and carry out deals not considered before. A prime example is the 2008 debacle, when

---

30 https://www.sec.gov/Archives/edgar/data/1571996/000157199617000004/delltechnologiesfy1710k.htm

Observations on M&A as a Growth Strategy

a. Corporate growth strategies and performance are greatly influenced by the **integrative, collaborative** or **consolidating** strategies such as M&As to foster innovation and deliver new customer value propositions. A focal firm can lock horns with uncertainty and commercialization of innovation to seek new demand, exploit new resources and partnerships, transform channels and customer relationships, and deliver a new customer value proposition —all this by **acquiring breakthrough technologies, competent engineering teams, and expanded user base.**

b. M&A activity flurry is the outcome of increased deregulation, privatization, globalization and liberalization adopted by several countries the world over. They are a potent tool to help expand product portfolios, enter new markets, acquire new technology, gain access to research and development, and gain access to resources. M&A is now an integral part of corporate strategy on account of modern deal design and antitrust regulation, as well as specific changes in business models and competition brought on by the shareholder value paradigm, digital revolution, deregulation and globalization. As stated by the CEO of Novartis, **"If you want to stay in the top league, you must combine."**

c. M&A can help a company grow significantly in a short span, to fill portfolio gaps, and boost long-run competitive advantage through synergies and economies of scale. It can also help create favourable future exit options (A large company with diversified revenue and customer channels is an attractive purchase proposition). Apart from enabling rapid growth, an acquisition may help the acquirer enter new markets and target new customer segments via the target's existing channels. An many forward-thinking players benefited from lower valuations during the fag end of the crisis, which helped them accelerate their businesses, pursue a broader range of deals, avail of non-cash structures, fresh capital, and benefit from high leverage—all this in times of recession.

Novel **strategic solutions** will help companies survive and thrive in today's challenging times of tight liquidity, grave uncertainty and ever-evolving, tech-driven business environments. Going forward, both parties in an M&A deal may necessarily need to rely on exhaustive valuation methods to manage risks and share rewards. They may need to prudently set financial banisters and scrupulously define boundary conditions. Accurate valuation is even more significant to acquisitions in volatile times, to achieve win-wins amid prevalent industrial lows and downturns.

3. Brand Value and the GPS Paradigm

In the modern-day business, the significance of brand value cannot ever be overemphasized. Corporates cannot ignore this vital element driving the sustainable success of any company. The GPS Paradigm puts a premium on value-added marketing as opposed to conventional marketing. Contrary to popular perception, brand management is not the sole concern of consumer-facing companies. Even the low-glamour players into heavy engineering, industrial tools, electrical components, and the like must create and cultivate strong brand recall values which alone will help them strike purposeful M&As across the globe. The GPS Paradigm helps them serve this crucial but underrated purpose through each of the G, P and S components. Under the tenets of ground intelligence, corporates need to necessarily think out of the box regardless of the spheres they operate in. A great deal of thought must go into building key messages and innovative marketing campaigns that are commonly seen only in the B2C spheres. Their specialized domains and functions cannot condone the explicit need to acquirer could specifically choose to expand their geographic footprint into new states or countries, by seeking to acquire a target based outside of their immediate geographic area. Alternatively, the acquirer can market products/services to a limited number of customers to access or attract new customers via a horizontal acquisition. Last but not the least, the opportunity for synergies between the acquirer and the target is one of the key advantages of an M&A strategy. Synergies may include greater efficiency, lower overheads and economies of scale.

d. The 2004 BCG Consulting Report contends that acquisitive growth strategies create superior shareholder returns. Successful acquirers choose acquisitive growth only when it is an inherent part of their strategy, and they are confident they can use it to create sustainable competitive advantage. Consequently, they deliver above-average returns and develop a detailed understanding of the role of M&A as a growth strategy long before the bidding. This way, capability gaps can be instantly bridged rather than wait to develop capabilities internally.

e. According to Bain & Company's 2019 Report, M&A transactions have increasingly become important value-triggers in the tech sector over the past decade, and will continue to be so in the years ahead. The tech deal volume has surged to $500 billion, growing 31% in the past five years. The three key factors fueling M&A in tech are: one, need for increased connectivity and advent of 5G creating demand for new products and better offers; two, an accelerated transition to cloud; and three, the need to access proprietary data such as high-precision location data. Also, tech innovation continues to shift from R&D in established companies to venture-backed start-ups, where risk convey their value props to the target audience in the form of powerful narratives. Close-knit partnerships can be formed with the core group of key customers such that the good word is circulated through their circle of influence. Digital platforms, key events and seminars, and reputed industrial publications must be judiciously exploited to tap potential end-customers through strategic communication narratives. Consequently, the whole chain from lead generation to deal closure can be optimized to the extent possible. The concerted effort can also open up hitherto untapped geographies for making smart and decisive inroads. Based on a strong brand connect with key customers, strategic decisions like identifying growth areas, employing value-based pricing, and consolidating market positions can be taken with more conviction and credence.

In the coming era, sustainable success would imply a ceaseless drive to probe the capricious minds of target customers, detect business risks and competitive threats as early as possible, fuel innovation, and develop strategic solutions for brand positioning and visibility to stay ahead of the competition with credible and compelling authority.

4. HR and the GPS Paradigm

The GPS Paradigm redefines the role of Human Resources (HR) beyond the realm of what the conventional parlance implies. More often than not, people issues rooted in bloated egos, thorny acrimony, and cultural conflicts are the key cause of many a failed M&As.

The GPS Paradigm redefines HR as a custodian of trust and catalyst of change, playing several critical roles – from analysing the respective work cultures, performing due diligence on differing management styles, remuneration aspects, and key synergies, identifying unifying factors and pain points, nipping conflict in the bud to the extent possible, conducting focused sessions for conveying the tolerance is higher. Consequently, more acquirers are targeting start-ups to gain access to their intellectual property, data and engineering talent. Recessions create new opportunities for M&A. The same was true of the 2008 downturn and will likely be just as true in current and future recessions. Lastly, given many cash-rich tech companies, the criticality of growth in technology and the entry of sovereign wealth fund investors in the tech space, M&A will be integral to any long-term strategy in technology. Companies will hence need to evolve their sourcing methods, perform due diligence on potential buys, and seamlessly integrate bought entities to extract the full value of inorganic strategies.

f. Deloitte's 2018 Technology M&A Report contends that the increasing pace of technological innovation will make M&A a good solution-centric strategy for accelerating product road maps, gain access to new technologies and markets, and outpace internal and external competitors.

g. According to an incisive ECONSTOR working paper by Rainer Frey and Katrin Hussinger, technological change is seen as one of the main drivers of merger activities. M&As can serve as an effective channel for technological restructuring or for strengthening technological core competencies. Further, overlapping research fields can necessitate the ownership of patents to continue research activities, and M&As can help acquire the patent portfolio of a rival firm. Also, firms can use M&As to enter new technology markets since diversification reduces risk. Moreover, a certain degree of technological diversification is necessary to keep pace with rapid tech developments; tech knowledge in ancillary fields coupled with distinctive core competencies enable firms to adopt and integrate technologies developed by value chains and rationale governing compensation structures, benefit schemes, and key people policies, effecting a smooth people transition towards the new scheme of things, and developing sustainable solutions for protecting the cocoon of shared vision, synergistic growth, and common objectives.

The GPS Paradigm calls for HR champions playing a strategic role, over and above their mainstream roles of employee recruitment, remuneration and retention. **And the involvement should begin right from the pre-deal phase. It is imperative that HR heads understand the intricacies of business, whether operational issues, financial aspects, production and productivity targets, market realities, competitive landscape, or the evolving paradigms and disruptions.** The GPS Paradigm assumes their proactive involvement in all the three tenets – Ground Intelligence, Unconventional Partnerships, and Strategic Solutions.

People risks are critical for both buyers and sellers, and typical pain points hover around culture conflicts, key employee exodus, leadership issues, compensation, and benefits acrimony. According to a Mercer survey report titled "People Risks in M&A Transactions", 55 per cent of the buyers foresee talent management to remain a key HR challenge in future M&A transactions.

Having ground intelligence on people is therefore key for any successful M&A; it is human intellect that structures unconventional partnerships and develops strategic solutions. People aspects of integration cannot be addressed in a silo. **Issues related to human capital and performance are inherent in, and critical to, every work stream. Those issues involve responding to questions such as: Have people from both sides accepted the rationale for the deal? Do they possess the skills necessary for the integrated organization to prosper over the longer term? Is the right talent being deployed** competitors. Knowledge in non-core technologies helps firms to spot emerging technological opportunities and latch on to new trends.

h. Big technology companies are now exploring M&A deals at the fastest pace in years despite increased regulatory scrutiny. This deal-making spree hints at a further consolidation of tech superpowers amid the COVID-19 crisis, as the groups look to capitalize on record valuations and resurface as the dominant players in emerging sectors. Tech companies are looking at the pandemic as the new normal and seeking attractive opportunities rooted in consolidation in sunrise areas.

in the right positions and will people be required to learn new systems, processes, and skills to do their jobs?

I recollect the prudent approach of a seasoned founder of a large textile company for whom I did a couple of mid-sized M&As aimed at strategic business expansions. He always sought detailed information on the CEO and CFO of the transferor company in every deal. He invariably regarded their key employees as the most crucial assets comprising the core knowledge, experience, skills, creativity, and motivation that can alone steer the said M&A deals towards fruition and fulfilment.

Chapter 4

Unleashing the M&A Force

Unlocking and unleashing the M&A potential, as I see it, calls for an exclusive approach that does not end with the mere professionalization of M&As or its acceptance as a key business strategy. In fact, there is no one formula or silver bullet strategy that can been identified as the key driver for any M&As in future. As mentioned earlier, the GPS Paradigm enables every company to thrive ahead than survive, staying relevant, and ensuring growth in the same breath. I have invariably found start-ups across the globe naturally ingrained in the GPS Paradigm mode of doing business. I am amazed at their freewheeling mindset and bold, inventive approach across diverse sectors, including fintech, edtech, healthcare, retail, media & entertainment. Unknowingly, they eat, drink and sleep the GPS Paradigm. Large & mid-sized companies, except a few, are unduly fixated on their day-to-day operations and rarely think beyond their routine businesses.

Let us now discuss each GPS component for M&As in greater depth

1. Ground Intelligence for M&As

Intelligence is the ability to adapt to change.

– Stephen Hawking

Ground intelligence manifests itself in a variety of ways as part of an M&A transaction, and can be called a part of the due diligence process before, during and after the deal, other than the routine legal, financial, technical, environmental, and reputational aspects. It implies those facts and information that are essential to the specific transaction, be it in terms of critical data, firm culture, operations to be integrated, potential opportunities, and the like. Ground intelligence is undoubtedly one of the key success factors in an M&A, especially in case of a cross-border transaction which most definitely involves the sensitive issue of integrating differing, and often conflicting, cultures.

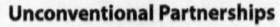

Norikazu Tanaka, head of Mitsubishi Operations, makes the pithiest observation in this context: "The most important key to success is the assurance of a global network, both internally and externally." Cross-border deals, he explains, necessitate the acquisition of knowledge on the ground. The engagement with local stakeholders from the internal global network including joint venture partners is critical, which alone helps mitigate risks and helps collect all critical information. A comprehensive knowledge of the given sector, he says, is elementary, which may include "anything from understanding what the future holds, what the likely trends in demand and supply are, to analyzing competitors and profiling customers."[31]

The technology boom has now seen companies increasingly relying on software tools to provide ground intelligence such as client's financial health and credit worthiness, as also trade credit risks in new countries.[32]

---

31   https://www.cliffordchance.com/content/dam/cliffordchance/PDF/Feature_topics/Cross_Border_Changing_World.pdf

32   https://www.tinubu.com/tinymcefilemanager/file/2013-10-18_10-14 f

Ground intelligence also includes information on emotional intelligence, which helps nurture an environment of co-operation through better self-awareness, social awareness, self-management and social skills during negotiations and post deal integration. Consequently, the emotionally intelligent workspace becomes even more attractive to prospective buyers and fosters increased cohesion and collaboration, which is influential in defining a company's qualitative metric.[33]

Ground intelligence ought to imply the collection of compelling data, that helps foresee future opportunities as well as obstacles, is key to success. Time spent in gathering and analyzing the information is time well spent.

The most important element of ground intelligence is to cover critical market information to determine options such as identifying potential targets, enlarging product range, cutting costs, and acquiring new customers. It can be gained by assessing the current market scenario, reviewing competitor strategies, and benchmarking competitive position.[34]

Last but not the least, cultural information is considered an imperative ground intelligence for a deal's success, given that seamless integration is a key factor leading to expected returns on investment. Cultural intelligence can be gathered both pre-merger and post-merger, via different modes like encouraging inter-team communication, finding out the cultural operation style of the acquiring/acquired company, adopting a global, macro-outlook and holistic attitude, and developing purposeful cultural training programs.[35]

---

33 https://www.smallbizdaily.com/value-emotional-intelligence-during-ma-process/
34 https://www.actisspartners.com/en/market-intelligence-in-ma-operations/
35 https://www.linkedin.com/pulse/why-cultural-intelligence-cq-key-skill-your-ma-team-needs-barile

2. Unconventional Partnerships in M&A

Be creative. Use unconventional thinking. And have the guts to carry it out.

– Lee Iacocca

Unconventional Partnerships

Ground intelligence **Strategic solutions**

Unconventional partnerships have become a strategic tool for growth, more so in the face of prolonged economic challenges, increased innovation, and growing sector convergence. The rise in consumer demand and a shift in their preferences and behavior have forced corporates to plan for multiple futures. Unconventional partnerships allow companies to avoid disruption, seek new sources of revenue and earnings, while cutting costs as well as bolstering their R&D processes.[36]

As stated by **Pip McCrostie Former Member of EY's Global Executive Board:** *"Those companies that best achieve commercial advantage through combining strategic M&A and cooperative responses to new challenges will be best positioned to win. Buying and bonding are now key features of the corporate growth agenda."*[37]

According to E&Y's 2016 Global Capital Confidence Barometer, companies are seeking growth opportunities outside their home markets, with investments in other countries, and 75% of respondents opting for cross-border growth.[38] These transactions are predicted

---

36 https://imaa-institute.org/global-capital-confidence-barometer-buying-bonding-alliances-join-ma-engines-growth/
37 Id.
38 Id.

to be a blend of joint ventures, minority investments, alliances and incubator-type investments. Research by Bain has revealed a remarkable growth in success stories of unconventional deals. Unconventional arrangements allow companies to build their capabilities and focus more on outcomes rather than on control.[39]

Further, unconventional partnerships are especially useful in times of economic downturn caused by the current COVID-19-imposed disruptions, sticky trade wars, and even political upheavals like Brexit.

BCG's 2019 M&A Report found that corporate audacity pays off, with success largely driven by acquisitions outside the buyer's core business segment. A paradigm shift in the deal objectives led by a technology revolution has ensured that the focus is not to gain control of a company but to gain access to specific capabilities, talent, technology, or partnerships. Technology is blurring industry boundaries and boosting sector convergence. As companies increasingly integrate technology into their products and services, complex ecosystems are emerging on the business landscape across industries. To bring together all the required elements of tech-enabled offerings, companies must now work with a far wider range of partners than in the past.

The conventional bilateral partnerships within a single industry are now passé. Instead, we are seeing more and more of multilateral cross-industry partnerships with supple ecosystems, calling for more deeper integration and subtle negotiations.[40]

---

39 https://hbr.org/2018/05/why-traditional-ma-is-becoming-less-important
40 https://www.bcg.com/publications/2019/mergers-and-acquisitions-report-shows-downturns-are-a-better-time-for-deal-hunting

3. Strategic Solutions for M&As

You've got to think about big things while you're doing small things, so that all the small things go in the right direction.

— Alvin Toffler

Unconventional Partnerships

Ground intelligence   Strategic solutions

A successful M&A transaction should necessarily go above and beyond in terms of outcomes. In the ultimate analysis, what is the purpose of strategic mergers and acquisitions? Beyond doubt, they must offer an innovative solution to a sticky or challenging business problem. An example of a solution could be an intention to start an altogether new product line, add additional facilities, enter a new market, or gain expertise in some critical business area, or acquire intellectual property. For professional services firms, a strategic M&A, more often than not, ought to be about gaining credibility, adding intellectual firepower, or changing the balance of power in a particular market.

The defining bottom line is that a strategic merger yields value for both the acquired and the acquiring firm.[41] Other M&A strategy solutions could be increasing market share by acquiring a competitor, adding service capability, or adding research capabilities or assets like a competent sales force.[42]

Strategic solutions demand a comprehensive growth analysis examining the target market for the combined product and solution portfolio. Having said that, in the short term, sales and marketing personnel may

---

41 *Supra* at 9.
42 https://pocketsense.com/difference-between-strategic-financial-mergers-4858.html

strive to quickly create new product bundles or solutions and identify product improvements for the pooled offerings.[43]

Robust information technology is must in the context of strategic solutions, especially of the post-integration variety. An efficient IT system unleashes synergies, integrates financial systems and customer data, enables cross selling, and reduces logistics cost.[44]

4. GPS Paradigm in Practice for M&As

Many companies have knowingly and unknowingly adhered to the GPS Paradigm in recent times, which has led to several game changing deals. These are companies that began life as start-ups but have now grown bigger than a century-old MNC. GPS Paradigm is their DNA!

Let us dissect a few prominent examples:

a. In September 2018, **Netflix** created the Post Technology Alliance with several camera equipment, editing, color correction, and encoding companies. The motive was to ensure that all participant products comply with Netflix's content specifications.[45] This was indeed a bold, unconventional move by Netflix towards maintaining market dominance. The offbeat partnership was indeed a strategic solution enabling Netflix to establish content supremacy.

b. Certain companies are now beginning to build their entire businesses around ecosystems. For example, Japan's **SoftBank Group** is developing a comprehensive system of subsidiaries

---

43 https://www2.deloitte.com/content/dam/Deloitte/us/Documents/mergers-acqisitions/us-ma-m-and-a-driven-sales-and-marketing-know-wehre-to-play-and-how-to-win.pdf
44 https://www.mckinsey.com/business-functions/strategy-and-corporate-finance/our-insights/understanding-the-strategic-value-of-it-in-m-and-38a
45 *Supra* at 46.

and making strategic investments in dynamic sectors such as telecommunications and technology.[46]

c. Many hospitals and health systems are increasingly opting for non-traditional collaborations to achieve a judicious blend of maintaining their independence while achieving the traditional benefits of consolidation. For instance, the Western Maryland Health System, Meritus Health, and Frederick Memorial Hospital jointly formed the **Trivergent Health Alliance Management Service Organization (MSO)** in 2014. The MSO helped reduce insurance denials by more than $3 million annually and ensured a shift in favour of weight-based dosing of antibiotics, netting annual savings of $2.8 million and improving the group's antibiotic stewardship. It also reduced supply costs by almost $3 million through a group purchase.[47]

d. From 1999 to 2004, **Oracle** consolidated 70 internal systems into a single Enterprise Resource Planning (ERP) system for all business functions, including sales and finance. This approach saved the company $1 billion annually and created a conducive platform for effecting an ambitious M&A strategy of more than 50 deals from 2005 to 2009. Consequently, Oracle can now integrate most acquisitions within a six-month time frame. This is a sterling example of using data to create a strategic post-integration solution triggering phenomenal efficiencies.[48]

e. Tech giant **Google** has struck various unconventional partnerships, which are now household names fetching it billions of dollars in revenue. Google has proven experience of working with alliance partners to create inclusive and universal products, unlike specialized software for limited

---

46 *Supra* at 46.
47 https://www.advisory.com/daily-briefing/2016/07/21/beyond-ma
48 *Supra* at 50.

minority use. It also shows a marked tendency to acquire small and flexible start-ups that can quickly adapt to its work culture, thereby be immediately recognizable as a "Google product".[49] Sterling examples of such strategic industry solutions include Android and YouTube, which helped Google to build an all-encompassing platform despite the contrary claims by many analysts.

f. **Facebook** has fully exploited its cash piles to take control over familiar sectors adjacent to its core product as a strategic solution for its consumers (WhatsApp for $22 billion) as also far-flung sectors (Oculus VR for $2 billion). Microsoft, Yahoo and Amazon have made similar big-ticket bets: Minecraft developer Mojang ($2.5 billion), Tumblr ($1.1 billion) and video game streaming site Twitch ($970 million), respectively.[50]

g. **Amazon** has entered into unconventional partnerships in areas as diverse as grocery chains. The $13.7 billion Whole Foods deal in 2017 was the company's biggest acquisition to date. It has also bought Zappos, a shoe retailer for $1.2 billion in 2009, Twitch, an e-sports streaming site, for $970 million in 2014 and Ring, a smart home system, for $1.8 billion.[51] These acquisitions have helped Amazon keep pace with every key trend[52], making the company an all-encompassing online retailer giant. In the words of Amazon's CFO Brian Olsavsky, they are *"looking for well-run companies with highly differentiated customer experience, and a real sense of customer obsession that*

---

49 https://www.allbusiness.com/what-do-google-acquisitions-reveal-about-strategy-10585-1.html
50 https://time.com/3815612/silicon-valley-acquisition/
51 https://marketrealist.com/2018/07/a-look-at-amazons-acquisition-strategy/
52 https://www.businessinsider.com/acquisitions-that-made-amazon-the-giant-it-is-today-2019-6?IR=T

matches ours."[53] The acquisition pattern suggests that Amazon's priority is enhancing customer experience to make inroads in as many markets and gain competitive edge.

It is apparent that companies that follow the GPS Paradigm **of M&As**, whether as part of a well-defined strategy or inadvertently, are well-set for achieving mega success. This is especially true for companies focused on technological innovation, given that data revolution today permeates every aspect of an M&A transaction, right from the pre-transaction diligence process to post integration intricacies. In today's ultra-competitive times, the only way to retain an edge is by ensuring unconditional flexibility, the ability and agility to cope with ever-evolving market demands.

Statistics tell the whole story of tech dominance in modern-day business acquisitions. Overall spending on tech acquisitions topped $170 billion in 2014, up 54% from the previous year and more than double the amount spent in 2010, according to PrivCo, a research firm that tracks investments in private businesses. As technology heavyweights grow in size, they seek strategic acquisitions for a dual purpose: **to broaden their businesses and to sustain the pace of innovation.** As stated by Peter Levine, a general partner at venture capital firm Andreessen Horowitz, "*Companies are buying innovation, and as large companies need to be competitive and want to increase their footprints in a variety of different areas, one of the best ways to do that is through acquisition.*"[54]

5. GPS Paradigm Triumphs: Sterling Examples of Leading Tech-Giants

Beyond doubt, the tenets of the GPS Paradigm have been a cornerstone for creating a well-defined M&As growth strategy aimed at mitigating

---

53   https://www.inc.com/guadalupe-gonzalez/amazon-acquisition-strategy-pillpack-jeff-bezos.html
54   *Supra* at 56.

risks, minimizing costs, and maximizing revenues, growth potential, and customer base, even if these tenets have been applied unknowingly, not formally as the GPS Paradigm.

It is for the benefit of the young guns among business leaders that I present a comprehensive study of three global tech giants – how they approached M&A and recorded unprecedented growth through strategic acquisitions. *It is pertinent to note that these tenets apply to companies across verticals, not just tech corporates or start-ups, given the fact that technology is as integral for tech companies as a product or service as it is for non-tech companies as an enabler. These companies, I repeat, commenced operations as start-ups and are now the face of the new world economy!*

1. Facebook

Over the years, Facebook carried out a number of acquisitions to improve its core website strategy in terms of programming talent, photo sharing, and advertising revenue. In parallel, it was also busy developing best-in-class app and mobile technology. Having said that, it was only after 2014 that Facebook achieved mega success; this was the time **Facebook began to pursue the most unconventional partnerships in absolutely uncharted territories.**[55] Let us take a closer at each of these key acquisitions:

a) WhatsApp (2014):

This was Facebook's largest acquisition to date, valued at $20 billion. **Acquiring a mobile messaging app broke new ground even as Facebook gained a huge chunk of overseas customer base in one stroke.**[56] Of the purchase price of $16 billion, $4 billion was paid in cash and $12 billion in Facebook shares. Facebook paid another $3.6 billion

---

55 https://www.investopedia.com/articles/investing/021115/facebooks-most-important-acquisitions.asp
56 Id.

as compensation to WhatsApp employees for staying on board. [57] At the time of acquisition, Facebook contended the deal would enhance its connectivity and utility value props and help user engagement across both companies. WhatsApp, on the other hand, would retain its brand and operate independently towards connecting over one billion people.[58] Facebook founder Mark Zuckerberg attributed the deal's success to its vast resources and infrastructure, a source of great value to its customers and advertisers.[59] It is pertinent to note that the deal revenue was monetarily counted as a loss; Facebook achieved exponential user growth: 1.5 billion users as of 2020, 70% among them active on a daily basis.

A critical valuation analysis concluded that the long-term value for Facebook shareholders would be positive. In terms of enterprise value, the billions of shared messages on daily basis justified the deal price tag.[60] **The principal benefits turned out to be WhatsApp's high user base across all age groups including teenagers and adults, which paled monetization into secondary significance.** The high volumes of data exchange created a global communication revolution.[61]

b) Oculus VR (2014):

This deal marked Facebook's debut into virtual reality, blending social networking with virtual gaming.[62] The $2 billion deal comprised $400

---

57 https://www.investopedia.com/articles/investing/032515/whatsapp-best-facebook-purchase-ever.asp
58 https://www.sec.gov/Archives/edgar/data/1326801/000132680114000010/exhibit991_pressrelease219.htm
59 https://www.digitaltrends.com/news/zuckerberg-to-tell-congress-that-instagram-whatsapp-needed-facebook-to-succeed/
60 https://pdfs.semanticscholar.org/7eed/1089b0b70e28be270860bd7e504f860d484f.pdf?_ga=2.146624502.394431081.1598205679-1342561433.1598205679
61 https://www.linkedin.com/pulse/facebook-acquisition-whatsapp-case-study-peter-kovac
62 *Supra* at 1.

million in cash and 23.1 million shares of Facebook common stock, with an additional $300 million earn-out in cash and stock. **Both companies hoped to deliver the world's best virtual reality platform in terms of social media, communications, gaming and entertainment powered by a transformative and disruptive technology.**[63]

MIT Technology Review found the acquisition a strategic part of Facebook's mission to build a "knowledge economy", besides heralding the future of computing. Mark Zuckerberg called the deal historic in the light of virtual reality's impending impact on everyday life. Market experts cheered the deal, anticipating mainstream acceptance for virtual reality given Facebook's mass-marketing appeal.[64] The acquisition fueled a spree of venture capital deals in VR and augmented reality, which tripled from the year 2014 volumes, the time when the deal was announced. Facebook's Midas touch validated the hi-tech sector and sent other companies into overdrive to vie for a place of pride. Oculus founder Palmer Luckey acknowledged that Facebook resources did wonders towards achieving the Oculus technology targets.[65]

c) Ascenta (2014):

Facebook acquired this British designer of solar-powered unmanned aerial vehicles for $20 million to take the Internet to developing countries.[66] **Zuckerberg contended the connectivity aircrafts, by virtue of the deal, would help beam the Internet from the sky besides aiding drone aerial and on-the-ground technology, more so in rural areas.**[67] Although the operations are largely shrouded in secrecy,

---

63   https://about.fb.com/news/2014/03/facebook-to-acquire-oculus/
64   https://www.technologyreview.com/2014/03/26/13732/what-zuckerberg-sees-in-oculus-rift/
65   https://www.vox.com/2016/3/24/11587234/two-years-later-facebooks-oculus-acquisition-has-changed-virtual
66   *Supra* at 1.
67   https://www.roboticsbusinessreview.com/rbr/facebook_acquires_solarpowered_drone_maker_ascenta/

Ascenta shared its intent of collaborating with NASA scientists on how to enable two-thirds of the world's internet-deprived population based on high-altitude aviation expertise.[68]

d) CTRL-Labs (2019):

Facebook bought CTRL-Labs to make inroads into the artificial intelligence market. CTRL-Labs excelled in building interfaces enabling users to control computers using their thoughts. The acquisition was in line with Facebook's augmented reality initiative using a brain-computer interface.[69] **The plan was to use CTRL's innovative inputs to significantly improve user experience.** The main appeal was a CTRL product called wristband measuring neuron activity, helping neural signals directly translate into digital signals without buttons or keyboards.[70]

Being emerging technology, there's inadequate research to help validate it, but one of the deal analyses found the devices a potential game-changer in the world of targeted advertising, poised to boost ad revenue while respecting ethical and privacy concerns.[71]

The deals elaborated above clearly reflect the Facebook intent, of acquiring companies both for their technologies and teams. **Over time, Facebook has carried out several strategic initiatives: from product consolidation to mobile development to a spree of acquisitions outside the core.**[72] **Facebook's penchant for unconventional partnerships and ceaseless innovation have helped it foray into hitherto unfamiliar markets.** Zuckerberg's M&A motive is to *"build relationships by establishing friendships with other company founders,*

---

68 https://www.ft.com/content/b8a6524a-b627-11e3-b40e-00144feabdc0
69 *Supra* at 1.
70 https://www.bloomberg.com/news/articles/2019-09-23/facebook-to-buy-startup-for-controlling-computers-with-your-mind
71 https://analyticsindiamag.com/facebook-acquisition-of-ctrl-labs-data-privacy/
72 *Supra* at 1.

which provides a competitive edge and helps due diligence move quicker, have an aligned vision which results in excitement about working together, believe in the product, use scare tactics for smaller business to help convince them to join a larger enterprise, and move fast in terms of due diligence to beat out the competition and be flexible."[73] **He rightly contends that the biggest risk in a fast-changing world is "not taking any risk".**[74] **Facebook's pro-risk strategy is unflinchingly focused on disrupting sectors and breaking boundaries.**

A valuation and market multiples analysis of Facebook's acquisitions of WhatsApp and Instagram (photo sharing app) firmly established that business integration helps achieve faster growth during the phases of growth stagnation. With the Instagram purchase, Facebook followed a horizontal growth strategy – of acquiring a potential competitor to increase users and dominate the smartphone application space. With the WhatsApp acquisition, Facebook assumed leadership position in the instant mailing sector by creating a social networking giant. [75]

Business integration as a growth strategy is aimed at gaining quick access to new technologies, the know-how, competent resources, and stronger market position. However, this strategy fails owing to cardinal errors at critical stages – where in analyzing the market, looking for possible target companies, or in trying to address the post-acquisition challenges of merging differing cultures and managements.[76]

This is where the importance of **ground intelligence** comes in. With authentic due diligence based on accurate ground information, the integration process becomes smooth and seamless. Business

---

73 https://www.businessinsider.in/tech/mark-zuckerberg-explains-facebooks-secret-for-acquiring-companies/articleshow/56656388.cms
74 https://www.grin.com/document/275569
75 https://www.researchgate.net/publication/320077051_Business_Integration_as_a_Strategy_of_Growth_in_the_Social_Media_and_Network_Markets_the_Case_of_Facebook/link/59ccb650aca272bb0510f4d4/download
76 Id.

integration is a consequence of globalization, dramatically accelerated by the Internet boom and greatly impacting the social media and network market, given better customer access to information and cut-throat competition among rivals. A thorough analysis of the environment is critical to tap the right growth opportunities and avoid needless risks. In this context of M&A, Facebook is a role model as it has achieved most of its defined goals post a scrupulous business integration. Facebook has proved time and again that strategic acquisitions help companies gain new users and keep potential competitors at bay.[77]

2. Google

Google's exclusive brand of acquisition strategy has made it one of the most successful tech giants in the world. Given an evolving digital world and burgeoning competition in the mobile and digital assistant space, **Google's multi-pronged approach to maintaining its dominance in its cash cow business of search and ads is very well defined and executed: adopt an acquisition strategy in the spheres of digital commerce, branded hardware products, and content; attempt to integrate services into every aspect of the digital user experience; seek new revenue streams in sectors with great market potential, namely the enterprise-side cloud computing and services. Google also explores industries ripe for disruption, including transportation, logistics, and healthcare.**[78] Let's summarize a few of the tech heavyweight's key strategic buys:

a) Android (2005):

Having acquired Android for a mere $50 million, Google captured over 70% of the operating systems market share. CEO Sundar Pichai acknowledged Android's capabilities in terms of creating

---

77 Id.
78 https://www.cbinsights.com/research/report/google-strategy-teardown/#conclusion

pro-consumer choice, flexibility and opportunity.[79] Google saw and hailed Android's dual contribution: a dramatic consumer choice boost and phenomenally improved mobile experience for users through a network of 39 manufacturers and 231 carriers in 123 countries.[80] The Android platform helps Google fetch a yearly revenue of $9.1 billion via Playstore, $7.5 billion via its search engine and $2.2 billion via Google Maps.[81]

A "toothbrush test", evaluating whether the acquisition impacted day-to-day life for the better and would be used at least once a day, found Android a ground-breaking acquisition. This deal was included among the best acquisitions of all time as it helped Google conquer the smartphone operating system space, one of the world's key product markets.[82]

b) YouTube (2006):

After having tried to make inroads into the video market with Google Videos, Google bought YouTube for $1.6 billion to garner a huge customer base to challenge the likes of Facebook.[83] Google maintained that the acquisition was a blend of a thriving online video entertainment community and Google's expertise in organizing information and creating new models for internet advertising. The transaction aimed to provide a more comprehensive user experience for uploading, watching and sharing videos, and enable professional content owners

---

79 https://www.blog.google/around-the-globe/google-europe/android-has-created-more-choice-not-less/
80 https://googleblog.blogspot.com/2011/08/supercharging-android-google-to-acquire.html
81 https://www.kamilfranek.com/how-google-makes-money-from-android/
82 https://webcache.googleusercontent.com/search?q=cache:UPfy9U-Va oJ:https://hbr.org/2016/06/ma-the-one-thing-you-need-to-get-right+&cd=29&hl=en&ct=clnk&gl=in&client=safari
83 *Supra* at 25.

to tap new audiences.⁸⁴ Google's share price rose to its all-time high post the acquisition, making it one among the decade's best performing stock. ⁸⁵

Hailed as the "best tech deal ever", it was stated that Google astutely joined hands with YouTube, its erstwhile direct competitor with a vast user base, to enhance its core business, boost ad revenues, map future growth strategy, and rule the roost in digital advertising. This deal transformed the online video sharing space and made it significantly consumer friendly.⁸⁶ An entrepreneurial analysis unfolded YouTube's power as the dominant online video provider with over one billion daily views, thanks to its user-friendly interface and focused marketing.⁸⁷

c) Nest Labs (2014):

Google enhanced its strategic foray into the 'smart home' space by adapting its Android OS to an Android TV system to provide a smart TV platform with interactive capabilities. As part of promoting this strategy, Google acquired Nest Labs to mark its debut in the home automation space of smart thermostats and smoke detectors. ⁸⁸ Google said it was "excited to acquire Nest to bring its amazing products to more homes in more countries." The all-cash deal was valued at $3 billion. Yet again, Google saw its share price soar post acquisition.⁸⁹

---

84 https://www.sec.gov/Archives/edgar/data/1288776/000119312506206884/dex991.htm
85 https://www.theringer.com/2016/10/10/16042354/google-youtube-acquisition-10-years-tech-deals-69fdbe1c8a06
86 Id.
87 http://mcl.usc.edu/wp-content/uploads/2016/07/11-Haiqiang-Wang_YouTube1.pdf
88 https://www.researchgate.net/publication/319631816_Strategic_Decision_Making_Google's_Acquisitions_Partnerships_and_the_Toothbrush_Test/link/59b6d925a6fdcc7415be6ae8/download
89 https://9to5google.com/2014/01/13/report-google-to-acquire-smart-thermostat-maker-nest-for-3-2-billion/

Nest now offers seamless integration of devices, thanks to the synergy with Google's current assets like artificial intelligence. Further, Google expanded its global reach by selling Nest products and combined products in an offer scheme. The outcome was the creation of an innovative automated home experience.[90] Google contends that Nest would help Google transit to ambient computing, creating a unified and cohesive consumer platform.[91]

Suranga C, a leading venture capitalist, has aptly observed: *"The firm's smartest acquisitions have been in areas where it had no special expertise, but were still close fits with the company's core search business, with Alphabet pushing into entirely new areas, from genomics and healthcare to autonomous transport."*[92] Google has clearly pushed the boundaries by venturing deep into artificial intelligence, and its cloud focus has been termed "valuable" by Alphabet, Google's parent company. Google has always sought partnerships with esteemed corporations to boost its competence in marketing, sales and engineering.[93]

Alphabet has always focused on acquisitions in its chosen spheres of cloud-based computing, artificial intelligence, virtual reality, hardware, and talent, besides striking strategic partnerships to fend off rivals. The new products act as a "moat", protecting Google's prime earner, now called Google Ads from disruption by boosting searches and improving customer experience. **Alphabet's modern-day approach to acquisitions can be summed up by founder Larry Page's famous "toothbrush test". In essence, a product or service needs to be used**

---

90 https://www.worldresearchlibrary.org/up_proc/pdf/1870-153923408522-30.pdf
91 https://www.theverge.com/2019/5/7/18530609/google-nest-smart-home-brand-merging-hub-max-rebrand-io-2019
92 https://www.wired.co.uk/article/google-acquisitions-data-visualisation-infoporn-waze-youtube-android
93 *Supra* at 25.

once or twice a day by customers and it needs to improve their lives, if Alphabet is to acquire the company.[94]

Numerous case studies have highlighted the astuteness of Google's global designs. Although many acquisitions are mainly within the native US, Google has penetrated other geographies through acquisitions to challenge established players, as also to enhance its products and services. Though some of its acquisitions like Motorola Mobility proved economically unfavorable, Google has effectively used M&A to expand its workforce, and enhance its products and services, setting the de-facto standard of acquisitions for others, including Facebook, Yahoo, Microsoft, and Amazon.

Google has made major strategic moves focused on providing variants of digital/internet services. Over the years, it has acquired various start-ups and established firms to become a global provider of information and telecommunication services.[95]

As an integral part of its acquisition strategy, Google first evaluates whether a company is a good fit for the desired aim. The focus is firmly on delivering a strategic solution that can be productized. Secondly, Google is mindful of cultural issues to ensure a seamless integration. Last but not the least, Google is decidedly pro-risk and defines losses as a necessary risk.[96]

3. Amazon

Following in the footsteps of other tech giants, Amazon has pursued diverse acquisitions as a growth strategy. Let us discuss the key ones:

---

94 https://medium.com/swlh/gafa-what-can-we-learn-from-their-acquisition-strategies-ac4523be70e5
95 *Supra* at 25.
96 https://investmentbank.com/googles-acquisition-strategy-lessons-from-the-giant/

a) Twitch Interactive (2014):

Amazon forayed into cloud computing by buying this video game platform and community. The $970 million all-cash deal seemed perplexing to many observers, but Amazon admirably cashed in on Twitch's fiercely loyal fan base to create new gaming services for the community.[97] Amazon CEO Jeff Bezos called broadcasting and watching gameplay a global phenomenon which Twitch contributed to in great measure. Twitch CEO Emmett Shear acknowledged the role of Amazon's goodwill in reaching growth targets faster vis-à-vis what was possible as an independent entity.[98]

A market analysis of the acquisition concluded that Amazon gained a foothold in the content broadcasting market and added game development to its already diverse portfolio. Amazon prudently entered the $30.4 billion US video game market. Adding Twitch services to its Prime benefits, **Amazon created a loyal customer base and made it integral to the digital lives of consumers.**[99] **The deal also enabled unique sponsorship opportunities, demographic-focused advertising, and faster ad monetization.**[100]

b) Whole Foods (2017):

The e-commerce giant acquired the grocery chain for **$14 billion to further its brick-and-mortar footprint, and strengthen grocery delivery capitalizing on Whole Foods' large and loyal customer base.**[101] Amazon contended that the acquisition would pursue the vision of making the organic Whole Foods affordable for everyone,

---

97 https://www.cbinsights.com/research/amazon-biggest-acquisitions-infographic/
98 https://www.businesswire.com/news/home/20140825005820/en/Amazon.com-Acquire-Twitch
99 https://www.buyboxexperts.com/twitch-the-unlikely-but-important-amazon-business/
100 https://techcrunch.com/2014/08/25/amazons-twitch-acquisition-is-too-big-to-fail/
101 *Supra* at 44.

with price drops and integration of Amazon Prime into the Whole Foods Market point-of-sale system.[102] Shares of Amazon zoomed up 3% post announcement, adding $14 billion to the company's value, wholly recovering the purchase price. Whole Foods' capital swelled, courtesy a 27% premium on share price.[103]

A critical evaluation of the deal identified multiple benefits. Amazon gained full-fledged entry into the billion-dollar grocery industry, besides an infrastructural boost. Prime customer benefits helped captured a vast user base challenging industry leaders like Walmart.[104] Further, the deal helped leverage the existing Whole Foods grocery footprint as localized distribution centers, with Amazon using its data to change store layouts, product offerings and integrating grocery buying with other applications like Alexa.[105]

c) Ring (2017):

Amazon acquired Ring for $1 billion, a Wi-Fi-enabled doorbell that streams live doorstep video to a smartphone or tablet, which enabled Amazon couriers to leave packages inside customers' homes.[106] CEO Bezos said, "They were buying Ring's market position, since its position and momentum is very valuable."[107] A Ring spokesperson remarked the partnership would form an innovative customer-centric company committed to reducing crime rates through better home security tools.[108]

---

102 https://press.aboutamazon.com/news-releases/news-release-details/amazon-and-whole-foods-market-announce-acquisition-close-monday
103 https://mnacritique.mergersindia.com/amazon-whole-foods-acquisitions/
104 Id.
105 https://www.imd.org/research-knowledge/articles/amazon-buys-whole-foods--a-grocery-revolution/
106 *Supra* at 44.
107 https://www.theverge.com/2020/7/30/21348483/amazon-jeff-bezos-alexa-ring-market-dominance-antitrust-hearing-congress
108 https://www.theverge.com/2018/2/27/17059664/amazon-ring-acquisition-smart-home-security-cloud-cam

A market analysis concluded that the acquisition would transform the highly competitive smart home market, given formidable rivals like Apple and Google, and add to Amazon's smart home portfolio.[109]

d) PillPack (2018):

The $753 million deal [110] acquisition of an online pharmacy home-delivery service, marked Amazon's long-awaited debut in healthcare. Share prices of several incumbent pharma companies dropped 10% on the news.[111] Amazon maintained that it would help PillPack make consumers' lives simpler and healthier, working hand-in-hand with the value chain to create a better pharmacy experience.[112]

A market analysis found the deal handy for Amazon to break into the highly competitive $500 billion prescription industry, thereby challenging medical stores and drugstores. Offering this services to Prime customers helped them tap a huge customer base, bolstering Amazon's drive of opening health clinics and improving medicinal research.[113] The deal was deemed "disruptive", slated to make Amazon a dominant player in the healthcare market.[114]

e) Kiva (2012):

This $800 million all-cash purchase of Kiva, an innovative warehouse and logistics player, revolutionized robot-assisted transport – helping

---

109 https://www.geekwire.com/2018/amazons-acquisition-ring-means-smart-home-market/
110 https://www.sec.gov/Archives/edgar/data/1018724/000101872419000004/amzn-20181231x10k.htm
111 *Supra* at 44.
112 https://www.businesswire.com/news/home/20180628005614/en/Amazon-Acquire-PillPack
113 https://www.cnbc.com/2019/05/10/why-amazon-bought-pillpack-for-753-million-and-what-happens-next.html
114 https://www.hcinnovationgroup.com/clinical-it/pharmacy/article/21072247/amazon-purchase-of-pillpack-poses-disruptions-of-healthcare-environment

move large shipments from one point to another.[115] Amazon maintained Kiva's technology would improve productivity by enabling employees pick, pack and stow goods faster. Kiva contended the association will lead to the creation of innovative material handling solutions.[116]

A key analysis called the deal "most transformative in Amazon's acquisition history", enriching Amazon with custom-made robots that reduce turnaround times, as also operating costs. Amazon's contribution to automation swelled market cap 8.5x times.[117] **A valuation analysis highlighted manifold benefits: enhanced logistics and supply chain network, faster deliveries and competitive edge, productivity boost, optimal manpower and better customer-centricity.**[118]

The above deals bear testimony that Amazon has judiciously used the M&A route to modify its businesses, as also tap new markets. This phenomenal success is the outcome of superior ground intelligence, which has helped Amazon keep track of every upcoming trend and earn revenues over $200 billion through diverse investments.[119] In fact, Morgan Stanley has predicted a high compounded annual growth of 16% for Amazon, highlighting its acquisitions as its fastest growing catalyst.[120] Unlike software companies who are focused on building product portfolios or buying customers through acquisitions, Amazon invariably eyes margin growth-yielding, low-profile market areas

---

115 https://www.businessinsider.com/acquisitions-that-made-amazon-the-giant-it-is-today-2019-6?IR=T
116 https://www.sec.gov/Archives/edgar/data/1018724/000119312512122135/d318297dex991.htm
117 https://pitchbook.com/news/articles/ma-flashback-amazon-announces-775m-kiva-systems-acquisition
118 https://www.sibmbengaluru.edu.in/wp-content/uploads/2018/11/2_Adoption-of-next-generation-robotics.pdf
119 *Supra* at 62.
120 https://www.forbes.com/sites/louiscolumbus/2018/04/22/5-acquisitions-that-will-fuel-amazons-next-growth-phase/#439d764f65ba

with high transaction volumes and undifferentiated channels. Many enterprise software acquisitions are consolidation-driven but Amazon is focused on building and extending new business models.[121] Amazon has also been experimenting with fintech initiatives, lending out small loans in developing countries, such as India and Brazil.[122]

Amazon CFO Brian Olavsky's statement: "We've changed, again, the automation, the size, the scale many times, and we continue to learn and grow there,"[123] proves its pro-risk strategy, a key common factor in its diverse acquisitions. **Founder Bezos aptly remarks: "A dreamy business offering has at least four characteristics. Customers love it, it can grow to very large size, it has strong returns on capital, and it's durable in time, with the potential to endure for decades."** No wonder Amazon has grown by leaps and bounds – from a humble internet bookstore to a powerhouse across retail, logistics, consumer technology, cloud computing, and media & entertainment sectors. Amazon is clearly adopting a proactive stance to fuel its AI and enterprise ambitions through the M&A route.[124]

The Boston Consulting Group (BCG) underlines the fact that for e-commerce and technology firms, acquisitions can "boost innovation, streamline operations and processes, shape customer journeys and personalize products, services, and experiences." Acquisitions help companies grow and serve as a strategic tool to internationalize their presence. Amazon has hence ventured into diverse markets like grocery retail, robotics, and gaming. Amazon's decision-makers have consistently tapped the potential of acquisitions to improve its products and services and develop markets. Acquisitions

---

121 Id.
122 https://www.greyb.com/amazon-business-strategy/
123 Id.
124 https://www.cbinsights.com/research/report/amazon-strategy-teardown/#acquisitions

are a vital contributor to Amazon's growing global dominance in e-commerce and beyond.[125]

4. Jio (2020)

One of India's best-known companies, Reliance Industries unveiled a detailed digital plan in 2020, under the stewardship of promoter Mukesh Ambani. In what was an undeniably depressing year marked by unprecedented havoc caused by a demonic virus, Reliance secured two top-notch investors – Google and Facebook – garnering over $20 billion in the process. The Google deal will help build an operating system suited to the needs of a cost-effective smartphone of 4G and 5G capabilities, while the Facebook collaboration will help small merchants in India reinvent their businesses. Independently, Jio Glass is intent on making mixed reality a success, notwithstanding the failed attempts of both its principal investors, Google and Facebook.

---

[125] http://opus.escpeurope.de/opus4/files/60/Workingpaper_Stefan_Schmid_Sebastian_Baldermann_2019_online.pdf

Chapter 5

Historical Trajectory of M&A

Those who do not remember the past are condemned to repeat it.

This dictum of Spanish philosopher George Santayana was popularized by British statesman Winston Churchill, although one of Churchill's original 'history' quotes is equally profound:

The farther backward you can look, the farther forward you are likely to see.

The high relevance of these quotes to the book's core makes them more pertinent than what their universal significance implies. History is replete with scores of perceptive reference points to help one unfold the essence, credence, tenets and intricacies of mergers and acquisitions (M&A), whether seasoned practitioners or budding professionals, veteran academicians or rookie students, business owners or advisors.

Before we look at the world's top M&A deals, we must examine the M&A trajectory over the years to trace its origins and evolutionary path so that we are better prepared to cope with, nay capitalize on, the onslaught of technological dominance going forward.

The oldest known standalone mergers — both landmark developments — were largely remedial initiatives to resolve trade conflicts and consolidate trading power for the reigning industry heavyweights. It is pertinent to note the circumstances of these milestone mergers:

1. The 1708 East India Company merger,[126] saw the original **East India Company** integrating with the **English Company Trading to the East Indies**. The latter was a parallel set-up floated in 1698 under a state-backed indemnity of £2 million. However, the stockholders of the original company subscribed for shares worth £315,000 in the new body and assumed dominant control. The ensuing trade conflicts between the two bodies ultimately made way for the merged entity which was rechristened the **United Company of Merchants of England Trading to the East Indies**, better known as the Honorable East India Company (HEIC). Although HEIC initially traded in commodities such as indigo, tea, salt, and cotton, it eventually sidelined its commercial objectives and virtually ruled India through military action and administrative control.

2. In 1821, the North West Company merged with the Hudson Bay Company.[127] Both these prominent Canada-based fur traders had long indulged in cut-throat competition that turned hostile and violent over time. The merger was effectuated through a massive asset pooling exercise, and the new set-up was rechristened Hudson Bay, which became the world's largest fur trading company of the given era.

The vibrant economy of the United States largely led the global M&A evolution, as it was on American soil that mergers were first explored as a business arrangement. This M&A trajectory can be best studied in terms of waves; each wave mirrors the ripples caused by differing economic, political, and legal factors of the respective time span. The defining attributes of each wave are summarized below:

---

126 https://www.hubert-herald.nl/BhaHEIC.htm
127 https://www.hbcheritage.ca/history/acquisitions/the-north-west-company

First Wave M&A (1897-1907)[128]

a. Mergers of this era were characterized mainly as "horizontal mergers"[129], where companies from the same industry consolidated to form a power sector.

b. These mergers were the outcome of the recession and heightened economic loss caused by the Great Depression of 1883;[130] consolidation thus became necessary for industrial and business resurgence.

c. The key mergers of this time period included JP Morgan's billion-dollar corporation United States Steel[131], created by buying out industrialist Andrew Carnegie and merging around 33 companies. This steel monopoly controlled almost 80% of the market share. Another striking example is the Standard Oil Trust[132] formed in 1882, a merger of oil producing and refining companies that transferred assets and interests to a holding company named New Jersey Company. This consolidation formed an oil monopoly, controlling about 90% of market share.

d. Since the economy was in an evolutionary stage at this point, the merger activity was limited to bustling industries such as steel, petroleum, and energy.

e. This wave scripted the unrestrained economic expansion and prosperity of prominent players in key sectors and also triggered the development of capital markets.

---

128 West Texas A&M University, https://www.wtamu.edu/~jowens/FIN6320/MERGER%20WAVES.htm
129 Id.
130 Id.
131 https://www.jpmorgan.com/global/company-history
132 https://www.britannica.com/topic/Standard-Oil

f. The end of this wave was marked by the advent of World War I as well as increased legislative scrutiny by way of the Sherman Antitrust Act, which restricted the combination of entities in violation of the competition law.[133]

Second Wave M&A (1916-29)[134]

a. This wave saw the rise of oligopolies, which were meant to counter the monopolies of the prior era, as well as to sidestep the fag-end stringent antitrust legislations of the first wave.

b. A good case in point is again the Standard Oil Trust; the New Jersey company was ordered to divest all its major holdings.[135] This wave marked a turning point as M&A shifted focus from core industries to other industries. The key players of this era came from the automobile space. Ford acquired the luxury car manufacturer Lincoln Motor Company for portfolio diversification.[136] This wave also made equity the prevalent finance source, ahead of cash.[137]

c. The stock market crash of October 29, 1929[138] brought the second wave to a screeching halt as economic activity suffered a lethal pause.

Third Wave M&A (1955-1975)[139]

a. This phase was dictated by diversification initiatives besides the creation of conglomerates.[140]

---

133 Tilberg University, http://arno.uvt.nl/show.cgi?fid=129395
134 Supra at 3.
135 Supra at 7.
136 https://corporate.ford.com/history.html
137 Supra at 8
138 Supra at 3.
139 Supra at 8.
140 Supra at 3.

b. These business arrangements primarily aimed at attaining economic prosperity in the aftermath of the stock market crash. Another key trigger was the strict enforcement of antitrust laws like the Clayton Act (which attacked unethical business practices such as price fixing and monopolies) and the Celler-Kefauver Act (which prevented mergers that could stifle market competition).[141] Further, diversified portfolios reduced financial risk as the security was provided by successful businesses from other sectors and led to creation of a robust internal capital market.[142]

c. A key example of the third wave conglomerate is General Electric, which had interests across various sectors like energy, transport, and electricity.[143]

d. A looming oil crisis signaled the end of this wave.

Fourth Wave M&A (1981-1989)[144]

a. A key development of this wave was the introduction of "hostile takeovers".

b. Besides the generic mergers, hostile takeovers became common in the aftermath of the stock market crash. There were a number of divested divisions available at a lower price for acquisition post the conglomerate wave. Further, financing now shifted from equity to debt due to the rise of "leveraged buyouts", which largely employed outside debt to acquire a company, and divested most assets post acquisition.[145]

---

141 Id.
142 Supra at 8.
143 https://www.ge.com/about-us/history#/
144 Supra at 8.
145 Supra at 8.

c. A disastrous example of this phase was Robert Campeau's hostile takeover of Federated Department Stores (FDS) on July 29, 1988. Campeau paid $8.17 billion for the company stock at a pre-acquisition market value of $2.93 billion. 97 percent of the purchase price was debt-financed. Less than two years later, FDS filed for Chapter 11 bankruptcy and Campeau was rendered jobless. In contrast, successful strategic acquisitions of this era included the Quaker Oats acquisition of Gatorade, General Electric's purchase of RCA, Wells Fargo Bank's acquirement of Crocker National, and KKR's buyout of Beatrice and Duracell.[146]

Fifth Wave M&A (1993-2000)

a. This ongoing wave, spanning almost five decades from origin till date, is definitively focused on global level concepts of cross-border mergers and mega mergers running into billions of dollars. Further, with the opening up of various economies across the world, M&A deals have hit a global high to become a popular option for several liberalized economies. Consequently, M&A activity has shifted from the erstwhile epicenter of US to other prominent markets across the globe. Besides, breakthrough tech innovations have triggered the emergence of entirely new and profitable sectors. [147] This wave, not surprisingly, has scripted and staged some of the world's most successful M&A (and unsuccessful) deals, which are discussed at length in the next chapter.

---

146 https://www.cato.org/sites/cato.org/files/serials/files/regulation/1997/4/reg20n2d.html
147 Supra at 8.

Chapter 6

Classic M&A Transactions at a Glance

Here is a snapshot of classic M&A transactions to highlight the fact how the tenets of GPS Paradigm were unknowingly applied to these deals.

1. **Dow Chemical-DuPont (Year: 2015, Sector: Science and Innovation)** **Purpose:** to fuel innovation in agriculture, materials science and specialty products divisions. The two companies gainfully made up for lost revenues from falling crop and oil prices, competitive pressure, and strengthening US dollar.
2. **The Walt Disney Company-21st Century Fox (Year: 2019, Sector: Digital Media & Entertainment)** **Purpose:** to make decisive inroads into the streaming services market in terms of viewer content and global reach. The expanded Disney portfolio and improved ad sales will help challenge streaming giants like Netflix.

3.	**CVS-Aetna (Year: 2018, Sector: Healthcare)**
	Purpose: to create a value-based healthcare giant, a fine blend of drug manufacture and health insurance.
	The deal created more opportunities for integrated care and value-based insurance design. The coordinated retail clinic expansion is likely to boost future cost savings.
4.	**Charter Communication-Time Warner Cable (Year: 2016, Sector: Telecom)**
	Purpose: to create one of the largest broadband providers and pay TV providers in the United States.
	It promised substantial cost efficiencies through synergies in purchases, overheads, product development, engineering and IT.
5.	**United Technologies-Raytheon (Year: 2020, Sector: Aerospace and Defense)**
	Purpose: to create one of the world's largest aerospace and defence companies.
	Although the profitability will unfold only in the long run, this deal is one of the highest in terms of deal value for the decade. Better research capabilities are expected to further strengthen defence capabilities going forward.
6.	**Google-Android (Year: 2005, Sector: Technology)**
	Purpose: for marking Google's entry into the potent space of smartphone operating systems, one of the world's most important product markets.
	Android was acknowledged not only for dramatically increasing consumer choice but also improving the user experience through a robust network of manufacturers and carriers across 123 countries.

7.	**Pfizer-Warner Lambert (Year: 2000, Sector: Pharmaceuticals)** **Purpose:** to create a global pharma corporation through leadership in both anti-hypertensive and anti-hyperlipidemia markets. The transaction diversified Pfizer's research and development portfolio, creating potent synergies for various types of drugs like insulin, diabetes, endocrinal and gastrointestinal disorders.
8.	**JP Morgan Chase-Bank One (Year: 2004, Sector: Banking)** **Purpose:** to emerge stronger in revenues, net income, card member services business, and market share. The deal helped JP Morgan ride over the pain of prior failed deals, as also the impact of the dot-com debacle and the debt burden caused by the telecom setback. The deal was a big boost to revenue, operating earnings, and total deposits.
9.	**Microsoft-Nokia (Year: 2013, Sector: Technology)** **Purpose:** to capitalize on respective synergies to unlock new connectivity and automation scenarios. It was written off in 2015. In 2019, a strategic collaboration between the two players has sought to accelerate transformation and innovation across industries with Cloud, Artificial Intelligence (AI) and Internet of Things (IoT).
10.	**Vodafone – Mannesmann (Year: 2000, Sector: Telecom)** **Purpose:** to create one of the world's largest mobile phone operators of the time. The acquisition has given the merged entity extensive wireless coverage in the European market. The combined entity at the time of the deal became the fourth largest company in the world in terms of market value after Microsoft, GE, and Cisco.

11. **Saudi Aramco-SABIC (Year: 2018, Sector: Oil)**

   Purpose: to make Saudi Aramco one of the world's largest petrochemical companies employing a long-term downstream strategy.

   The deal helped Saudi Arabia's economy soar high on the wings of its global oil trading operations. Saudi Aramco is now one of the world's largest petrochemical companies with a production volume of 90 million tonnes.

Chapter 7

Unfolding the JV Core

As a corporate lawyer, structuring JVs and foreign collaborations has been my passion all along, a trait I inherit from my senior, R. A. Shah (More about him in the next chapter), and whilst working on several JVs over the years. This is truly fascinating work, if you enjoy meeting businessmen, decision makers, founders, and CEOs from diverse sectors to hear them unfold their vision, aspirations, thought processes, points of view, sharing experiences on other JVs, holding marathon discussions, zeroing in on key issues, strategizing the way forward, drafting, negotiating, and eventually seeing them kick off their new arrangements before embarking on yet another voyage of discovery and deliberation.

In my journey of over 30 years, I have designed the structure of over 150 JVs and alliances in various forms across diverse industries. I fondly recollect classic examples of large Indian pharmaceutical and retail clients for whom I had the privilege and pride of structuring a series of JVs which have today made them giants in their own sectors. In the process, I have learnt and understood the intricacies and peculiarities of diverse businesses, including pharmaceuticals, retail, manufacturing (auto, cement), and services (IT, education, engineering, healthcare).

Joint ventures, to my mind, are nothing but quasi-partnerships structured in the form of an incorporated company (what is today known as LLP in India). Why company? Because it was the sole earliest known form in India which could have limited liability. In India, therefore, an incorporated company with limited liability offers a well-defined format ably supported by the various provisions of the Indian Companies Act, 2013 (erstwhile Companies Act, 1956). The Joint Venture Agreement provisions are also incorporated in the Memorandum of Objectives and Articles of Association to reflect the share ownership (51:49, 50:50, 74:26, 90:10), management (board of directors, process for holding meetings including special quorum and veto or affirmative rights), roles & responsibilities of partners (including transferring or licensing of brands, technology, manufacturing, research or local administration), transfer restrictions on shares (preemptive rights or right of first refusal, put and call options), process for deadlock resolution, exit provisions including termination & non-compete, representation, warranties and indemnities, and arbitration.

Provisions of the Shareholders' Agreement (SHA) or the Joint Venture Agreement (JVA) are legally enforceable against the shareholders (as being contractual obligations) and by virtue of including the provisions of the SHA/JVA in the Articles of Association also against the company.

Along with the SHA or JVA, other ancillary agreements are structured depending on the contribution of partners which include transfer or licensing of intellectual property (trademark/technology/deputation of technicians), toll or contract manufacturing (more in the context of Indian pharma companies or items reserved for small scale manufacturing), marketing & distributorship or franchise agreements, export agreement, local admin support agreement for regulatory compliance, and various support agreements with regard to technology platforms.

1. JVs and the 1991 Economic Liberalization in India

In 1991, India opened up the economy and allowed foreign direct investment in what was then called as the 'automatic route' (implying the elimination of the need for approval). Foreign companies were allowed to invest up to 51% ownership in 34 select industries and were also permitted licensing of technology against a lump sum fee of USD 2 million plus royalty of 5% on domestic sales and 8% on exports; and additionally, a royalty of 2% on exports and 1% on domestic sales for use of trademarks. Consequently, between the span 1991-1996, the global theme became 'Destination India' by choice. Every foreign company wanted to set up joint venture in India and many founders of large and mid-sized Indian companies travelled abroad to secure a good foreign company as investor-cum-technical collaborator. In majority of those MoU/Term Sheets executed during that period, the Indian founders blindly committed technical fees 'as per Indian laws'. They genuinely believed that they were obliged to pay royalty of 5% and 8% for technology as per Indian laws. But in reality, the business model itself could not afford payment of such royalties in many cases. Unfortunately, many Indian promoters who travelled abroad during that period did not seek proper guidance and ended up in messy situations.

> *Multinational companies usually are well advised by their internal business development or team of dedicated in-house counsel and they would make sure that they engage local lawyers to understand local laws, regulatory regime and also local business practices before entering into any alliance for doing business in other jurisdictions.*

The term joint venture or foreign collaboration although acquired a whole new meaning post 1991, foreign companies were successfully doing business since the pre-Independence era. Here's an enduring slice of history featuring some of the reputed business names of the said time frame:

Abott, 1901 – one of the country's oldest and most admired healthcare companies

Siemens, 1922 – the company's long-term commitment in India began in 1867, when Werner von Siemens personally supervised the setting up of the first telegraph line between London and Calcutta

Unilever, 1888 – visitors to the Kolkata harbour were delighted to find crates and crates of Sunlight soap bars, embossed with the words: "Made in England by Lever Brothers". With those crates began an era of Fast-Moving Consumer Goods (FMCG). Soon after, Lifebuoy was introduced in 1895, and other famous brands like Pears, Lux, and Vim. Vanaspati were launched in 1918, and the now ubiquitous Dalda brand was introduced in 1937. **Unilever set up its first Indian subsidiary Hindustan Vanaspati Manufacturing Company in 1931,** followed by Lever Brothers India Limited (1933) and United Traders Limited (1935). These three companies merged to form Hindustan Unilever Limited (HUL) in November 1956; HUL offered 10% of its equity to the Indian public, being the first among foreign subsidiaries to do so.

Bata, 1931 – The Swiss-domiciled Bata Shoe Company was set up in West Bengal and was later shifted to Batanagar. Batanagar was the first manufacturing facility in the Indian shoe industry to receive the ISO 9001 certification. The company listed its securities to public in 1973.

Colgate, 1937 – this was the time when handcarts were used to distribute the now celebrated Colgate Dental Cream Toothpaste.

Cadbury, 1948 – it began its operations in India through chocolate imports. On July 19, 1948, Cadbury was incorporated in India.

These and many foreign MNCs have been successfully operating in India across diverse industrial sectors, armed with technology, brands, research & development, and international management skills. En route their voyages, they would have entered multiple successful and unsuccessful JVs and business alliances.

In a joint venture, two or more businesses or organizations come together to share their competence, expertise, or resources to achieve a common goal. This coming together is governed by contractual rules for reaping the rewards of the alliance and bearing the risks involved. What then distinguishes a joint venture from other forms of partnerships like M&As? On the one hand, partners in a joint venture

The newer forms of JVs may be totally different from the traditional business models which were more driven by investments, products, brands and marketing, and research capabilities. Instead, these forms of JVs would be focused on value added areas, including access to customer data and intelligence, sharing of technology platforms for delivering products/services, 3D printing and robotics for manufacturing, and access to research and development for achieving technological breakthroughs.

maintain their separate legal identities; on the other, they share equity, liability, and profits governing their alliance through contractually binding agreements.

Before we move to comprehending how the GPS Paradigm is tailor-made for new-age JVs, here is a JV fact file for putting JVs in perspective.

2. Structuring Joint Ventures

Joint Venture is nothing but a glorified partnership of two business entities to pursue certain set objectives. **A substantial part of the structuring depends on the 'true' objective for which a joint venture is proposed.** Broadly, following are the reasons why companies would go in for a joint venture:

- **Desire to become or remain a market leader** in a particular product/industry/services, or desire to diversify into new areas with the help of any well-established partner.

- **Access to technologies/new products/markets/research & development (R&D):** for example, a lot of Indian pharma companies in earlier days did not have research & development capabilities and hence opted for JVs to acquire the said capabilities.

- **Risk-sharing or limiting capital investment** in areas which are highly capital intensive: for example, infrastructure like power, roads, and ports.

- **Reducing costs** of manufacturing and other overheads including expenditure on R&D.

- **Make the most of complementary skills/resources:** for example one party may have manufacturing base, whereas other might have strong marketing/distribution or IT network,

- **Making inroads into new markets:** for example, a foreign company may want to penetrate and establish their products in **new markets of other countries** with the help of local partners, or where the local laws do not permit 100% foreign ownership as was the case for certain industries like insurance, defence or banking in India prior to 1991.

The aforesaid objectives are merely illustrative and not exhaustive. Depending upon the current position of any business, future goals, technological advancement, and new competitive products or services, a company may decide to strike a strategic alliance or a joint venture. The key steps in this direction comprise the following:

- Identifying the right joint venture partner
- Identifying strategic & operational goals
- Execution of Memorandum of Understanding (MoU)/Term Sheet/Letter of Intent (LoI)
- Due diligence (legal, financial, technical & reputational)
- Preparing documentation (SHA/JVA) and closing
- Formalities post execution

But what's the proverbial starting point, one may ask. How does any company or founder/CEO embark upon the journey of setting up a joint venture? Who should take the lead? What's the exact process involved? What about Binding vs. Non-binding MoU/Term-sheet? When and how to choose external consultants, including investment bankers and lawyers to draft and negotiate the deal? What precautions should one take during negotiations? How does one focus on closing? What are the post-closure obligations? What if there are any red-flags, or parties hit a deadlock during the negotiations? What is meant by deal fatigue?

These are some of the key questions I will attempt to answer in the guiding light of my experience till date.

In today's context, when things are changing, and changing rapidly leaving little time to react, I would think every company should have a core intelligence wing comprising of internal and external trusted advisors to identify new opportunities and engage with potential collaborators.

Joint ventures are initiated by the companies on their own or identified through investment bankers or business associates. Many companies have their own market intelligence to identify business opportunities or needs. It is absolutely essential that founders or CEOs ensure an extensive network and hard market intelligence on customer preferences, competitors and their products, investors, technology, raw materials, and regulatory regimes. They must stay intimately connected with investment bankers and other professionals through industry chambers, associations, international conferences, and industry exhibitions. In other words, they must be aware of the pulse of the industry! They must be open to feedback and be ever ready to explore sunrise opportunities. Depending on the nature of discussion and exchange of information, the parties should execute a non-disclosure agreement (NDA) to make the discussion more formal and confidential.

What's the exact process?

Joint venture discussions are focused on 'business opportunities or needs', always held between the key decision makers from both sides.

Depending on the need, senior managements from respective parties or external consultants also get involved. To ensure structured meetings as also to attain quick progress, I feel it is imperative that the parties should, on priority, set out the following **strategic** and **operational** goals and other key issues demanding amicable resolution.

Strategic goals:

- To define **objectives** (whether the JV would be for manufacturing, or simply marketing, or for any other purpose)

- **Key contribution** from the respective partners, and **on what terms?** For example, royalty for technology, trademarks, marketing, manufacturing cost, supply of raw material, research & development, sharing of revenue on technology platforms, etc.

- **Management structure** including number of board members, who would be responsible for key decisions, appointment of CEO, chairman, etc.

- **Exit** options or rights

Operational goals:

- **Day-to-day management** and operations of the company, including secretarial & legal compliance

- **Internal practices & policies** for manufacturing, marketing/distribution, including reporting requirements, and

- Audit and **information rights**

Here, I must mention my experience of representing a mega German pharmaceutical company which entered into a joint venture with a large Indian company in the textile business. I recollect having shared my concern with the German company about the future of the joint venture, that pharma was not a core sector for the Indian company, and that it was only banking on one senior professional with the requisite domain knowledge of pharma. The German multinational conceded to my view but went ahead to forge a 51:49 equity owned joint venture solely based on the reputation of the Indian company as a premier industrial house. Right from the beginning, the strategic goals of both partners were starkly different, and it was a foregone conclusion that the Joint venture was heading towards termination, which did happen within five years. Co-incidentally, I was the counsel representing the Germany company for setting up the joint venture, as also for buying out the stakes of the Indian partners.

How Detailed Should the Term-Sheet or MoU Be?

According to me, there is no hard and fast rule about the form or substance of any term sheet or any memorandum of understanding (MoU). Term sheet should ideally capture the **'basic commercial understanding'** in simple and clear English. Also, in case a key point is missed or there is some development, an addendum or supplementary, term sheet should be executed to make it comprehensive. More importantly, ambiguity should be avoided on all issues, unless of course it is consciously done.

The parties must deliberate and agree upon all strategic and operational issues and execute a formal Memorandum of Understanding (MoU)/ term sheet. These are different names with the common objective of capturing the exact commercial understanding of the broad form of partnership including contributions by partners, and the way forward or process that would be followed to accomplish the objectives. **In some cases, exclusivity obligation is imposed for, say 90 or 120 or 180 days, wherein parties are bound not to entertain or talk to any other parties on the same proposal, and not to share confidential information. That is the reason why it is important to have a binding term sheet, but a lot depends upon the intention of the parties.** I would strongly recommend spending adequate time in internal deliberations to draft this core document as it is the reference point for all further negotiations and the way forward.

Ideally, the draft of this term sheet or any MoU should be prepared in consultation with lawyers (preferably trusted advisors) who understand the depth and width of business collaborations. **In my experience, most MNCs do not execute or exchange even one page of email on business unless discussed with their lawyers. In sharp contrast, most Indian companies, small firms, and start-ups rush to execute the initial document without commensurate thought or deliberations. They feel the clause 'subject to the internal discussions or board approval' will protect them, but this is a flawed notion. The plain truth is that if you make some commitments in the term sheet, it becomes next to impossible to retract during final negotiations.**

How and Why to Engage External Consultants?

Given the complexity of business models and structures, it is necessary to engage competent professionals who are the trusted advisors and consultants right from the formative stages of discussions and take their inputs before committing to anything, even if it is subject to further approvals. It is like deciding to construct a tower without seeking the expertise of an architect or environmental expert. In my experience, majority of the executed term sheets or any MoU that were devoid of comprehensive internal deliberations or consideration of external perspectives have invariably led to difficult negotiations subsequently.

Formation of a joint venture is a very important function that demands utmost care and precision. **Many multinational companies in Europe and the US have an exclusive internal experienced department to handle M&As, and JVs manned by in-house M&A lawyers.** Although smaller companies or start-ups may not have the luxury of having in-house M&A lawyers, I would strongly advise them to engage external lawyers who can share their unprejudiced perspectives and varied experiences to make the structuring and negotiations foolproof and conclusive. **Structuring or negotiating a joint venture is not a one-time transaction, wherein you buy or sell any asset or argue your case before any court of law. It is about creating the road map of a future business relationship keeping in mind your long-term objectives including succession planning etc, and hence it is extremely important to get the help of experienced hands ideally trusted advisors who can anticipate sticky issues in advance and construct mutually acceptable and feasible solutions.** I would think the time, money, and effort spent during the structuring phase is essential and worthwhile to ensure either a long-term relationship or a seamless exit.

Here, I would like to share an extremely interesting joint venture handled by me. I was representing a foreign textile company in a joint venture of 51% ownership (along with licensing of technology and key global brands) with an Indian company with manufacturing capacities. The JV was obviously lopsided in favour of the foreign company with majority directors, exhaustive veto rights, and the right to buyout in case of dispute. During the negotiations, the Indian company decided not to engage any external lawyers and rely on in-house advice. After a few months, the same Indian company approached me to represent them in another joint venture with a foreign company. The company secretary happily told me that he had used my previous draft (of the first joint venture) and had only changed the name of the foreign partner.

In the second joint venture, the Indian company decided to retain 51% ownership with majority rights. Since the company secretary merely changed the name of the foreign company and all earlier rights applied as before, it resulted in conferring substantial rights in favour of the foreign company, despite the fact that the Indian company was to hold 51%. When I read the document and pointed out the blunder caused by an erroneous use of a precedent, the company secretary had to face tremendous embarrassment before the senior management. I have seen many people committing such gaffes and then cutting a sorry figure on critical clauses. It is most important to understand that one may know the concepts of these clauses, but they may have to be carefully tweaked to suit the exact requirements, a flair which develops only with proven experience.

Who Should Lead the Discussions?

There is no hard and fast rule as to who should initiate the discussions; however, I would strongly recommend parties to set up two or three teams for the said purpose. It so happens that **if the topmost decision maker is involved right from the beginning, he or she tends to say 'yes' or 'no' instinctively and instantly. This may prove counterproductive or even fatal to the negotiations as there is no time for the top individual to make hindsight reversals, reservations, or even reflection,** and too much time is unknowingly spent on trivial and minor issues. If the second or third line of professionals or external counsel are involved in the discussions, it is always easier for them to take time to reflect upon and revert after due consideration. Also, they can always dodge difficult issues by submitting that they cannot take decisions at their level. This ploy is often the best way to borrow good time. Internationally, the Chairman or the CEO steers clear of participating in most negotiations but is duly informed and updated on every interaction by the team.

What if There Are Red Flags or Deadlocks During the Negotiations?

It is indeed possible that negotiations may take a longer time than anticipated towards concluding the deal or closing the transaction documents. It is also possible that parties may be stuck on critical issues in searching for an amicable or mutually acceptable way forward. In my experience, this happens when both parties are contributing equally to the joint venture or have almost equal stakes. If the joint venture is one-sided, the minority partner on feeling threatened often seeks extraordinary protection, making the discussions unduly strained. Hence it is important to strike the correct balance that offers right returns to the contributing partner, while taking the minority partner into confidence. Here, the objective of the joint venture becomes extremely important, not what individual partners get in the bargain. It is also possible that post implementation, due to new circumstances or change in law, an edge or an extra commercial benefit accrues to one partner. This is the pet point of conflict, and it is necessary to identify such potential conflicts upfront and agree upon a clear road map to resolve issues in a commercially viable manner.

For example, in one 50:50 joint venture, the American partner – a reputed home care products company – agreed to lend its global brands only for marketing the JV company products. The Indian partner agreed to enter into toll manufacturing and supply products to the marketing JV on an agreed cost basis. The marketing JV miserably failed because the Indian partner claimed compensation for unutilised capacity; it was also accused of padding overheads. I feel this is a fundamental flaw rooted in conflict which surprisingly the parties did not anticipate while structuring the joint venture. Fortunately, both partners amicably decided to quit the JV.

During negotiations certain basic assumptions may change due to internal or external factors, or partners may change their internal goals and decide to alter the position. This development may lead to friction or confrontation and may even bring the discussions to a grinding halt. It is therefore necessary to anticipate these critical issues or possibilities like referring certain issues to the senior-most person from both the sides to ensure a green signal. This is where the experience of all concerned – including the team of lawyers – plays an important role in one, anticipating issues and two, finding innovative solutions to iron them out in mutual interest, and show the way forward.

What is Deal Fatigue?

I have seen many JV transactions linger on for days and months without closure. Either the initial negotiations don't get concluded, or the due diligence process goes on and on post the term-sheet execution, or the documentation is not completed due to unexpected developments, or the discussion simply go off-track in hopelessly tangential directions. I have seen many joint ventures getting concluded in the shortest possible time while there have been cases which have dragged for more than a year or two only to be eventually aborted. **There comes a stage during negotiations when the deal neither gets done nor abandoned, either due to a commercial issue or hard negotiations during the documentation stage. This is the deal fatigue stage when the parties don't show the requisite keenness to conclude or move fast.** In my experience, the only thing that matters is the intention of the parties to proceed with the matter. If the intention is clear and definite, the fatigue can be wiped out, else it stays put to the detriment of the JV.

Joint Venture Agreement

Broadly, there are three basic models of JVs, each tailored to serve an underlying purpose:

Model	Salient Features & Suitability
JV as Distinct Entity *Complete autonomy but highest responsibility for desired outcomes*	• Reporting structure distinct from parents • Separate HR, facilities, and independent supplier management.
JV as Dependent Entity *Shared resources and accountability*	• Identified as a business unit of a parent • No separate HR
JV as Mutually Dependent Entity *Best of both worlds*	• Dotted-line-reporting relationships to parent organization

1. Business Plan

It is imperative that a fairly detailed and comprehensive business plan be drawn up prior to closing the deal. Now, this is easier said than done.

It may be easy to prepare the inaugural draft business plan, but given the fluid assumptions and objectives, it is difficult to make subsequent changes to it. More often than not, one partner (for varied reasons) stands to benefit more out of the JV than the other. This skewed plan could later lead to massive confrontation. Hence, **a no-holds-barred interaction between the parties – respective management heads as also the appointed JV champions – is must to collectively decide the JV milestones and timelines, capex, financials — all of which find refection in the foolproof business plan. Not preparing a business plan or avoiding detailed discussions on the same proves fatal. During its preparation, many unforeseen commercial issues may surface, which in fact would help the parties to make well-informed decisions.**

2. Equity Participation and Capital

What should be the percentage of equity participation of the partners in any JV is a commercial decision, and a matter for the partners to decide and negotiate. Having said that, it also has a crucial legal element to it. For example, a shareholder with 75% or more of the issued and paid-up capital has almost complete control over the company, including the power to pass special resolution under Section 114 of the Companies Act, 2013 (certain critical matters like alteration of capital clause, memorandum and articles, merger & amalgamation require 75% voting). This would be a case where a partner bringing most of the capital, products, and sophisticated technology may want to retain full control over the company, and hence asks for 75% equity participation. A shareholder with 51% and above has effective control over the company, as it allows for passing all ordinary resolutions in his or her favour, including resolutions to appoint and remove directors or increase share capital. A shareholder holding less than 50% but more than 25% will have the power to block all special resolutions, including crucial resolutions like amendments to articles or issuance of further capital to non-members, and reduction of capital. A holder of 10% or more of the paid-up capital would be entitled to make an application for conducting investigation into the affairs of the company or apply under Section 241 of the Companies Act, 2013.

Normally the partner who contributes the most in terms of capital, technology, brand name, trademarks, manufacturing, and the like would want to have at least 51% majority equity control over the JV. If the contributions are equal, the joint venture is structured on equal basis. In case any partner wishes to be play a minor role, he or she ends up taking 26% or even less.

3. Composition of Board

A company has two organs: a general body of shareholders and a board of directors. Rightly a shareholder having say 75% ownership will want to have majority directors on the board, so also 51% shareholders. However, in my experience, in many cases, I have seen an equal board representation, even when the shareholding is divided on 51:49 basis. Similarly, a shareholder holding more than 51% may want to have his or her own nominee as the chairman and managing director. It is also not uncommon to have the 51% decide the chairman and the 49% shareholder to choose the managing director, with the consent of the majority shareholder (consent not to be unreasonably withheld). In a 50:50 venture, the board is usually equally divided and the position of managing director is mutually decided upon. This aspect is crucial and must be thought through carefully before accepting any position. In short, the structure of the board directly depends on the shareholding pattern, but it is not uncommon to have different board structures.

4. Control and Management of Day-To-Day Operations

JVs call for exceptional maturity, especially in matters of control and management. So, the partners to a JV must exercise prudence in fixing the control issue. If the contribution by a partner is critical, say in terms of intellectual property, key resources, or breakthrough technology, that partner's dominance is justified and should not be challenged, unless it gets unduly dictatorial. Fixing 'control' is easier said than done. No partner would like to accept dominance of the other for the life of any JV and rightly so. In such situations, I have seen JVs negotiated for fixed terms, with an option to extend the term or to buy the subservient partner. However, this is not as easy as it appears as it needs an in-depth understanding of the basic ingredients of a joint venture. A fine temperament (read cool head) along with fine talent is absolutely crucial.

Partners having no experience of management should ideally avoid seeking such rights, as the same would make them accountable in case of default or failure to achieve success. This is a very important point and needs to be evaluated carefully. I would strongly recommend that ideally, JVs should have an independent and experienced professional as CEO/MD reporting to the board.

Astute risk management, due disclosures, and scrupulous performance management are critical to any organization's success. Ditto for the JV which must have comprehensive audit processes and reviews in place, and a strong finance department with an integral connect with the parent boards.

It is normal in any joint venture having foreign shareholders to delegate the day-to-day operations of the company to the local partner. However, decisions on crucial matters are only taken at the board meetings with affirmative consent of both the partners. I have seen some of the joint venture agreements giving a detailed management structure, namely the formation of the board, formation of committees, reporting requirements and the like.

In the 1990s, at a time when India was flooded with JV propositions, majority of the JVs were based on technology, products, and brands of the foreign companies. The Indian partners agreed to provide admin and local compliance support. Such arrangements inevitably house an inherent conflict as, at some stage, the partner putting in substantial contribution invariably wants commensurate compensation in addition to the equity dividend. This situation invites bitter conflicts culminating into acrimonious exits, which did happen during the 1990s era. To avoid such unpleasant situations, cost allocation methods and their basis should be decided beforehand by the JV organization.

5. Conflict Resolution

In the global scenario with multiple layers of business models, business leaders would have to exercise extraordinary patience and foresight to align people with different working styles, experience, and ambitions. Managing human capital is going to be a daunting challenge.

Often, top managements do not pay enough attention or spend adequate time in identifying thorny issues. In my experience, JV teams, at times, avoid taking a stand on such matters as they perceive it to be a negative beginning. Worse, a few issues are even swept under the carpet to avoid even a semblance of confrontation. In many cases, basic assumptions change, and priorities and objectives get realigned which lead to conflict. As mentioned above, it is therefore advisable to draw up at least a business plan of three to five years and stay focused on the core purpose identified for the formation of the joint venture. Either the purpose of JVs may get defeated or fulfilled. The outcome must be acceptable to all partners and in the event of the purpose being defeated, they must end the relationship in mutual interest.

Conflict invariably arises because decisions are taken to conform to the individual goals of partners. It is extremely important that decisions are taken in the 'interest of the joint venture' which may or may not be aligned to the individual interests of the partners. It is imperative that that key decisions makers of the JV are truly independent, at least the CEO.

Contribution from partners with (assured or agreed) returns should also be agreed upfront, else there is always a chance of conflict. In many cases when the JV starts benefiting one partner (maybe for diverse reasons) the other partner may hesitate to contribute even if he or she may have agreed upfront. The GPS Paradigm leaves no room for such conflicts to arise, leave alone intensify.

6. Contribution, Role & Responsibilities of JV Partners

Contributions by partners need to be reflected into the joint venture agreement and if necessary, a detailed separate agreement should be negotiated for the purpose. For example, **separate agreements should be executed for trademark licence, technology licence, manufacturing, marketing & distribution agreement, and export obligations. Most importantly, it should be made clear as to what would happen to those agreements post termination of the joint venture agreement. This is very tricky situation and needs to be thoroughly evaluated, discussed and agreed upon.** Typically, post termination of the joint venture, the continuing partner should agree to pay a fair compensation for services under these agreements to the outgoing partner if he or she happens to provide them.

On the face of it, fixing roles and responsibilities for the JV appears to be an easy proposition, but the real-world dynamics make this job a formidable challenge, particularly when you are dealing with new-age technologists. It is therefore necessary to appoint independent professionals with a proven track record. Strong domain knowledge and a rich and varied experience of prudent conflict resolution are equally critical. The choice of the CEO merits careful consideration as the leader must be capable of constantly willing to learn, be flexible to adapt, motivate and lead all teams towards the fulfilment of the stated JV objectives. Most importantly, the CEO must be free of bias in approaching and confiding in the parent boards. All partner organizations must be taken into confidence, strictly avoiding discriminatory conversations based on prior rapport or undue influence. The CEO and team must hold detailed discussions with the boards of the parent organizations to gauge their aspirations, priorities, and objectives to develop the final business plan, clearly specifying the goals and milestones collectively arrived at.

7. Minority Protection

A minority shareholder will always try to protect his or her interest in addition to statutory protection accorded to him or her under the Companies Act. Giving a minority shareholder veto rights on certain key items or a seat on board is very common. The list of the items on which the minority shareholders should have veto is often a contentious issue to negotiate. **Whenever I have acted for a minority shareholder, I have insisted on having "tag along" rights in favour of the minority shareholder. At the time of exit by the majority, he or she thus obtains valuation like a majority shareholder, which is otherwise not possible. I would think a minority shareholder should certainly negotiate good rights but should not reduce the majority to a minority or neutralize his driving position. As I said, the best way is to secure a good exit.**

As per the foreign exchange regulations in India, foreign investment is restricted to 24% equity ownership in companies which are classified as small-scale industrial units. Foreign investors who take 24% equity also seek extensive veto rights literally making it a 50:50 joint venture.

8. Transfer Restrictions

The most discussed and negotiated part of any joint venture in my experience are the provisions with regard to pre-emptive purchase of shares or what is commonly called as the right of first refusal or 'ROFR'. The simplest form of ROFR is a shareholder proposing to dispose his or her shares, who is obliged to offer the same to the other shareholders to purchase the same at a price to be decided by the selling shareholder, or to be mutually decided upon or decided by an independent valuer. However, every such clause is thoroughly negotiated on price and timing depending upon the strength of the partner. Next to ROFR are the provisions with regard to "tag-along" or "drag-along" rights. Tag-along right enables a shareholder to require the other shareholder (selling shareholder) to sell his or her shares and compels the selling shareholder to sell the shares of the other at the price realized by the selling shareholder. Drag-along right, on the other hand, enables a selling shareholder to drag the other non-selling shareholder and compel him or her to sell along with the selling shareholder. In view of the Supreme Court's decision in the case of *V. B. Rangaraj vs. V. B. Gopalkrishnan* (reported in AIR 1992 SC 453), the provisions with regard to transferability must be incorporated in the Articles for the same to be enforceable amongst the shareholders.

9. Deadlock Resolution

Often a "deadlock" is misunderstood as "dispute". A deadlock is nothing but a difference of opinion or disagreement on commercial matters or key matters. For example, one partner may think expansion of capital is necessary for the business, whereas the other may think raising money through debt would be an ideal solution. One may want an expansion or diversification of activities and other may not. It is possible that both parties may be right in their own analysis and therefore the crucial question is who should have the final say and if not, what the process should be to make both agree to a amicable solution.

In case of a deadlock, under the Indian Companies Act, 2013 either party may ask the court to dissolve the company, or in majority of such cases the courts in India have asked the party with majority ownership or control to buy out the other at a fair and reasonable price.

In addition, there are a number of alternatives available to parties to effectively resolve a deadlock. A casting vote to the chairman may avoid deadlock but may not offer an ultimate solution. Another method that has been tried in England is to submit the resolution on which there is a deadlock to a binding arbitration of someone who has sufficient knowledge of the business. In England some people also have tried to appoint an additional director called as 'swingman' director for the express purpose of resolving board deadlock or to grant a small shareholder a balancing vote. Some American State laws, e.g., California Corporate Code, authorize a court in certain circumstances to appoint such a director. In India, the most common way out is for parties to provide that the respective Chairmen of both the parties would settle the issue in the interest of the joint venture company, which may not necessarily be in the interest of the joint venture partners.

Cooling off mediation – Here, both parties agree to mediate till a solution is reached, failing which the onus is on the mediator to make a feasible decision.

Deterrence – Here, both parties accept the fair price as decided by an independent valuator. Deterrence also implies a penalty imposed by the partner who seeks the exit. This penalty can be in the form of a lock-in undertaking assuring that the interest in the JV would not be sold for a mutually agreed period.

The most common method recommended to resolve deadlock these days is to provide for the "Russian Roulette", wherein any party could make an offer to buy or sell shares at a particular price and upon notice sent to the other party. The party in receipt of the offer can either accept the offer or reverse it at the same price. Since the option to acquire or buy vests with the other party, the party issuing notice has to be careful and objective in determining his or her buying or selling price. In my experience this works best, and no one dares to trigger the Russian Roulette mechanism. This method is brilliant and ruthless in the same breath.

Texas shoot-out: Also known as the Mexican shoot-out, this arrangement has each party stating the buyout price only to a neutral referee in sealed bids. When the bids are disclosed by the referee, the highest bidder is declared the winner, claiming the right to buy out the loser's share of business.

Deadlock resolution is a complex clause and needs a deeper understanding of business models, roles and responsibilities of partners and their aspirations. As I have duly elaborated in the last chapter, I spent quality time with my senior, Mr. R. A. Shah, in structuring various options of deadlock resolutions for several Indian and foreign clients. The key here is first to understand the client, his or her vision, thought process, aspirations and, most importantly, strengths and weaknesses. It is imperative to understand all possible options and fallout situations, deliberate upon each option in great detail, and foresee the consequences. This is a cumbersome and tiring exercise but extremely crucial as it is wiser to take an informed decision for shaping your destiny rather than have the decision 'decided' by your destiny.

10. Non-Compete During and Post Termination

Typically, every shareholders' agreement or joint venture agreement would carry a covenant about parties agreeing not to compete during the existence of the joint venture and for a contractual period of say three to five years post termination. The pivotal provision of law on this point is Section 27 of the Indian Contract Act, 1872 (Contract Act), which provides that a contract in restraint of trade is void. Essentially, Section 27 provides that every agreement by which anyone is restrained from exercising a lawful profession, trade or business of any kind, is to that extent void, **except the agreement not to carry on business of which goodwill is sold.** In view of this clear law, the courts in India have taken the view that every agreement by which anyone is restrained from exercising a lawful profession, trade or business of any kind, is to that extent void, unless it squarely falls within the exception.

However, the Supreme Court in the case of *M/S Gujarat Bottling Co. Ltd & Ors. versus The Coca Cola Co. & Ors. (AIR 1995 SC 2372)* distinguished between restriction contained in an employment contract and restrictions contained in any commercial contracts like franchise agreements, and enforced the negative covenant running post termination, although the underlying principle governing all contracts in restraint of trade was the same. The Supreme Court analyzed and discussed the scope of Section 27 as under:

"Every agreement by which any one is restrained from exercising a lawful profession, trade or business of any kind, is to that extent void.

Exception 1 – One who sells the goodwill of a business may agree with the buyer to refrain from carrying on a similar business, within specified local limits, so long as the buyer, or any person deriving title to the goodwill from him, carries on a like business therein: provided that such limits appear to the court reasonable, regard being had to the nature of the business."

The said provision was lifted from Hon. David D. Field's 'Draft Code for New York' which was based upon the old English doctrine of restraint of trade, as prevailing in ancient times. The said provision was, however, never applied in New York. The adoption of this provision has been severely criticized by Sir Frederick Pollock who has observed that *"the law of India is tied down by the language of the section to the principle, now exploded in England, of a hard and fast rule qualified by strictly limited exceptions."* While construing the provisions of Section 27, the High Courts in India have held that neither the test of reasonableness nor the principle that the restraint being partial or reasonable are applicable to a case governed by Section 27 of the Contract Act unless it falls within the exception."

Despite the aforesaid, the Supreme Court relied on the observations of *Lord Morris in Esso Petroleum Co. Ltd. v. Harper's Garage (Stourport) Ltd., 1968 Ac 269* wherein the judge said: "These are helpful expositions provided they are used rationally and not too literally. **Thus, if A made a contract under which he willingly agreed to serve B on reasonable terms for a few years, and to give his whole working time to B, it would be surprising indeed if it were sought to describe the contract as being in restraint of trade. In fact, such a contract would likely be for the advancement of the trade."** [p.307] **These observations indicate that a stipulation in a contract which is intended for advancement of trade shall not be regarded as being in restraint of trade.** In Esso Petroleum Co. Ltd. (supra) the question whether the agreement under consideration was a mere agreement for the promotion of trade and not an agreement in restraint of it, was thus answered by Lord Pearce: Somewhere there must be a line between those contracts which are in restraint of trade and whose reasonableness can, therefore, be considered by the courts and those contracts which merely regulate the normal commercial relations between the parties and are, therefore, free from doctrine." [p.327] "The doctrine does not apply to ordinary commercial contracts for the regulation and promotion of trade during the existence of the contract, provided that any prevention of work outside the contract, viewed as a whole, is directed towards the absorption of the parties' services and not their sterilization. Sole agencies are a normal and necessary incident of commerce and those who desire the benefits of a sole agency must deny themselves the opportunities of other agencies."[p.328]

In the same case, Lord Wilberforce has observed: "How, then, can such contracts be defined or at least identified? No exhaustive test can be stated – probably no precise non-exhaustive test. But the development of the law does seem to show that the judges have been able to dispense from the necessity of justification under a public policy test of reasonableness such contracts or provisions of contracts as, under contemporary conditions, may be found to have passed into the accepted and normal currency of commercial or contractual or conveyancing relations."[pp.332-33] There is a growing trend to regulate distribution of goods and services through franchise agreements providing for grant of franchises by the franchiser on certain terms and conditions to the franchisee. Such agreements often incorporate a condition that the franchisee shall not deal with competing goods. Such a condition restricting the right of the franchisee to deal with competing goods is for facilitating the distribution of the goods of the franchiser and it cannot be regarded as in restraint of trade."

11. Transfer Restrictions

It is important to understand the jurisprudence around enforceability of transfer restrictions and voting rights contained in the shareholders' agreement or the joint venture agreement. Landmark judgment on this issue came from the Supreme Court of India in the case of V.B. Rangaraj vs V.B. Gopalakrishnan and Others (reported in AIR 1992 SC page 453) wherein the court observed that *"a restriction which is not specified in the Articles of Association is not binding either on the company or on the shareholders."* Further, the Supreme Court accepted the proposition of the parties that an agreement between two shareholders of a private company, by which restrictions are imposed on their ability to transfer the shares, may be unenforceable unless the same are incorporated in the Articles of the company. The Supreme Court relied on the following propositions, namely, in Re Swaledale Cleaners Ltd. (1968) 1 All ER 1132 it was held that it is well-established that a share in a company is an item of property freely alienable in the absence of express restrictions under the Articles. This view is reiterated in *Tett v. Phoenix Property and Investment Co. Ltd. and Ors. 1986 2 BCC 99, 140.*

The Supreme Court also relied on the commentary given in *Chapter 16 of* **Gore-Browne on Companies (43ʳᵈ Ed.)** dealing with transfer of shares and stated *"that subject to certain limited restrictions imposed by law, a shareholder has prima facie the right to transfer his shares when and to whom he pleases. This freedom to transfer may, however, be significantly curtailed by provisions in the Articles. In determining the extent of any restriction on transfer contained in the Articles, a strict construction is adopted. The restriction must be set out expressly or must arise by necessary implication, and any ambiguous provision is construed in favour of the shareholder wishing to transfer;* in **Palmer's Company law (24ᵗʰ Ed.)** *dealing with the 'transfer of shares' it is stated at page 608-9 that it is well-settled that unless the Articles otherwise provide, the shareholder has a free right to transfer to whom he wills. It is not necessary to seek in the Articles for a power to transfer, for the Act (the English Act of 1980) itself gives such a power. It is only necessary to look to the Articles to ascertain the restrictions, if any, upon it. Thus, a member has a right to transfer his share/shares to another person unless this right is clearly taken away by the Articles.* In **Halsbury's Laws of England (4ᵗʰ Ed.) para 359** dealing with 'attributes of shares' it is stated that "*a share is a right to a specified amount of the share capital of a company carrying with it certain rights and liabilities while the company is a going concern and in its winding.*

The shares or other interest of any member in a company are personal estate transferable in the manner provided by its articles and are not of the nature of real estate." Dealing with 'restrictions on transfer of shares' in **Penington's Company Law (6th Ed.) at page 753** it is stated that shares are presumed to be freely transferable and restrictions on their transfer are construed strictly and so when a restriction is capable of two meanings, the less restrictive interpretation will be adopted by the court. It is also made clear that these restrictions have to be embodied in the Articles of Association.

12. Voting Rights or Pooling Agreements

A question is often raised about the enforceability of the voting rights contained in the Shareholders' Agreement or any Joint Venture Agreement. The Bombay High Court in the case of *Rolta India Ltd. vs Venire Industries Ltd.* reported in [200] 100 Company Cases page 19, observed that a pooling agreement may be utilized in connection with the election of directors and shareholders resolutions where shareholders have the right to vote. However, **pooling agreement could not be used to supersede the statutory rights given to the board of directors to manage the company, the underlying reason being that the shareholders cannot achieve by a pooling agreement that which is prohibited to them if they are voting individually. Essentially, the court observed that the directors are fiduciary to the whole community of shareholders and not to a particular set of shareholders and therefore have to act in the interest of the company as a whole.** In the very same judgment, the court has also noted the fact that the American courts have accepted that directors are fiduciaries of various constituencies in the corporation. With the companies issuing shares to employees and workers, and also to set off creditors, the American courts have accepted that in the company there are various constituencies like shareholders' constituency, workers' constituency, creditors' constituency, etc. At the same time the American courts have also observed that the fiduciary relationship occupied by the directors requires the exercise of duties and attention to the best interest of the company and its entire body of shareholders, and hence any agreement which comes in the way of directors' fiduciary duty would be unenforceable, or at least the courts would be slow in enforcing the same.

US: Revised Model Business Corporation Act (RMBCA) – As per Section 7.31 of the RMBCA, a voting agreement is valid if it is not subject to any contractual defenses, and that the agreement would not be void or voidable under the applicable state's contract law. If the agreement is validly executed, any party to the agreement can sue for specific performance of the agreement if another party refuses to abide by the agreement. If a suit for specific performance is successful, the court will order the parties to vote the shares in accordance with the voting agreement. In the case of *Ringling Bros. v. Ringling*, dated 1999, three major shareholders had agreed ahead of time, to vote in five of the seven directors, and if they couldn't agree on the fifth director, their attorney would arbitrate and decide the fifth candidate. The court held that this agreement was entirely legal. Even though they had passed on their voting rights to a third party, which is generally impermissible, the bestowing of such a right was merely nominal.

In 2018, the Delaware Court of Chancery, in the case of *Schroeder v. Buhannic Chancery*, invalidated action taken by the holders of a majority of the common stock of a Delaware corporation to remove and replace members of the corporation's board of directors and management. The court observed that a provision granting stockholders right to remove directors might be valid if contained in a corporation's certificate of incorporation or bylaws but not in a stockholders' or voting agreement.

Another landmark case is *McQuade v. Stoneham*, dated 1934. In this case, the New York Court of Appeals held that an agreement, which contractually restricts the director's discretion and preclude them from acting in the best interest of the corporation and all shareholders, is against public policy. A shareholder agreement, which sterilizes the board of directors of a corporation, is not enforceable.

Canada: The Canada Business Corporations Act (CBCA) governs shareholding agreements (Section 145.1) which confirms that a written agreement between two or more shareholders may provide that in exercising voting rights the shares held by them shall be voted as provided for in the agreement. In 1960, a landmark judgment by the Supreme Court of Canada named *Ringuet v. Bergeron* observed in a clause wherein the shareholders agreed to vote so that each would be a director and would be appointed to a particular office. The court stated that shareholders entering into agreement to vote unanimously and observing such agreements is legal; at the same time it was held that the fiduciary relationship occupied by directors requires the exercise of duties and attention to the best interests of the company and its shareholders. It was accordingly held that the discretion of the directors to act in the administration of the affairs of the company cannot be fettered by such agreement.

Germany: According to Germany's securities law regulations, pooling/voting agreements can be entered into by shareholders, who are termed to be "acting in concert". Pursuant to statutory law, in either case acting in concert requires coordination among shareholders on the exercise of voting rights (first alternative) or collaboration of shareholders in another manner with the aim of bringing about a permanent and material change to the corporate strategy. In 2018 (II ZR 190/17), the Federal Court of Justice clarified for the first time that the coordination of shareholder behavior in an individual case does not qualify as acting in concert. According to them, the question of whether coordination among shareholders is limited to an "individual case" is to be determined applying a formal rather than substantive test. Second, mutual coordination of conduct among shareholders does not constitute acting in concert if it is aimed at maintaining an existing corporate strategy (or defining it for the first time), rather than at bringing about a permanent and material change to an existing corporate strategy.

13. Documentation

A good document is no substitute for a bad partner! And negotiating a joint venture is not about relentlessly arguing your case before a court of law. Having said that, I have been all along reinforcing the criticality of good documentation to all my clients who engage me for preparing and negotiating a joint venture agreement. I strongly believe that a good document is the one that creates confidence and builds trust amongst the partners. **The choice of words is crucial – the language must be simple, unambiguous, and respectful. There is no point in winning an argument while drafting a particular clause, which partners would love to hate, or which may create (often fatal) discontentment and discomfort throughout the negotiation span. I have seen many lawyers aggressively pushing their drafts, although discernibly not suitable for the given situation. Many law firms field junior lawyers to negotiate the draft joint venture agreement who may not have the requisite experience to handle critical clauses, particularly the management structure or provision concerning conflict resolution.** I strongly believe that adequate domain knowledge of the given industry and a thorough internal discussion with clients before participating in (and jumping to conclusions during) negotiations are absolutely essential. A good, seasoned, and mature lawyer can quickly and conclusively help create a congenial environment of trust amongst the partners long before the commencement of the joint venture.

I spend substantial time with my clients in understanding their points of view or perspectives while also sharing my experience of other joint ventures. This two-way street of interaction helps reach a consensus in good time, identify key positions that need to be defended at all cost, and build workable Plan B and C on hard positions.

Ideally, the document must scrupulously articulate all provisions in a transparent manner. The onus is on the person drafting the JVs to be fair to all partners while keeping every kind of bias at bay. I recollect an interesting experience in this context where I was representing Bayer AG in negotiating a JV with an Indian partner. The negotiations were led by their senior in-house M&A Counsel who was very particular about tracking even the minutest of changes to the document before it was sent to the other side. The purpose was to ensure 100 per cent transparency in documentation. These are seemingly small things of monumental significance that create the very foundation for congenial, purposeful, and solution-centric negotiations.

14. Conclusion

The structuring of any joint venture requires a thorough understanding of the commercial aspects of business as well as the implications of various legal provisions on the position of the joint venture partners, shareholders, and board nominees. The jurisprudence about the role of the shareholders and nominee directors in joint venture companies is yet evolving in India, so also in other parts of world. **Notwithstanding the prevailing uncertainties regarding a few provisions, joint ventures and strategic alliances are beyond doubt popular growth models regularly adopted by companies across different industries. The real challenge is before the legal experts and other professionals in finding mutually beneficial solutions to many complicated and convoluted issues within the four corners of law.**

Chapter 8

Unleashing the JV Force

1. Joint Ventures

JVs have been in existence since time immemorial. Literally thousands of JVs or alliances must have been formed in the past 100 years and equally must have got even wound up. In the United States, their use began with the railroads in the late 1800s. Throughout the middle part of the twentieth century, JVs dominated the manufacturing sector. By the late 1980s, they increasingly appeared on service industry horizon even as businesses looked for greener pastures for expansion and diversification into new areas.

JVs became even more common in the late 20th and early 21st centuries, when many industrially efficient nations saw many public and private JVs to construct hospitals, mass transit systems, and technology-driven projects. Even in developing countries, JVs spearheaded by foreign governments and nongovernmental organizations undertook many developmental initiatives of public good.

JVs are often formed between public sector and private sector firms. Better known as public-private partnership JVs, their purposes can be varied – whether infrastructure projects, scientific research, health initiatives, or community development. These arrangements typically employ private money towards the fulfilment of public goals. Many are set up for new ambitions, for managing risk in uncertain markets, sharing the cost of large-scale capital investments, and injecting newfound entrepreneurial spirit into maturing businesses.

Joint ventures have the potential to restrict competition, especially when they are formed by businesses that are otherwise competitors or potential competitors. They can also reduce the entry of other players into a given market. This is precisely why regulators regularly evaluate joint ventures for violations of antitrust law.

With the advent of information technology in the 1990s and its transformational evolution, we are riding high on the phenomenal advancements in Internet of Things (IoT) and other path-breaking technologies like AI, robotics, 3D printing, and machine learning. In the 1990s, the Internet essentially worked as a remarkable tool to improve communication, calculations, data storage, mining, and analysis which in turn brought about several business efficiencies. The Internet also provided excellent support for the formation of strategic joint ventures to enhance customer reach and tap new markets.

However, the Internet of Things (IOT), AI, robotics, 3D printing, machine learning, and the like are not merely a means to improve business or efficiency; they are proactively helping companies develop new business models for joint ventures or collaborations. **In the next 10 years or even prior, when these technologies would move up further in the value chain of evolution, most companies across sectors and spheres might have to altogether reimagine and reconstruct their business models, not just remodel their products like how they are gainfully doing today.** It is not difficult to foresee why and how many players may even become redundant if they fail the litmus test of this frenetic tech-led disruptive innovation.

The newer forms of JVs may strike a judicious blend of traditional players strong in their mainstream spheres and new-age companies promising better customer reach, new markets, and key resources based on changing consumer trends and preferences. We may see these collaborations

across all sectors – whether medicine & healthcare, education & sports, travel & tourism, media & entertainment, construction & housing, or banking & insurance. These JVs will combine engineering & manufacturing competencies with innovative services or solutions of disruptive nature to create new consumer experiences in all spheres or even may create a new market space altogether.

Future business leaders would need to envision the future of their enterprises and adopt the GPS Paradigm literally on a day-to-day basis given that technology is changing on an hourly basis!

In the earlier era too, business models were linked with technological developments, but the business models were separate from technology. That is not the case today. Now, technological innovation itself defines and decides the business models because it significantly, if not solely, addresses the multifarious challenges like identifying target customers, engaging with their needs, delivering measurable value, and monetizing the same. Prior business models were essentially capital-driven, today they are technology-driven. Technology (3D printing, robotics, and social media) is already leading the transformation in manufacturing, marketing, and product development. We now have specialized firms working hand-in-hand with major corporations, not merely as technology vendors but as technology partners working on revenue-sharing or profit-sharing arrangements. Going forward, technology wizards would undoubtedly play a key role as partners in large global industrial conglomerates as they already enjoy the unconditional backing of specialized private equity players.

As mentioned in the introductory section of this book, the tenets of the **GPS Paradigm of M&As** extend to joint ventures & collaborations (JVs) as well. Both modes are an integral part of business restructuring in the corporate world. Such business restructuring is led by both immediate and ultimate business objectives, as chalked out by corporate leaders, board of directors, and the strategic or dominant shareholders who design the strategic blueprint by exerting their influence or interest in the company.

To stay relevant in the extra ordinary competitive market, we may see newer forms of business restructuring, quasi JVs, or innovative commercial arrangements for profit sharing or pooling of resources between unconventional partners towards developing strategic solutions.

Going forward, irrespective of the form of restructuring, success in business would depend upon the ability of the corporate leadership to envision the future and act upon it with exceptional agility. Every form of business restructuring has its pros and cons; the onus is on the decision makers to carefully evaluate and choose the most appropriate form in the specific context of the foreseeable future, as also the desired outcomes. Towards this effect, the principles and prescriptions of the **GPS Paradigm** would undoubtedly prove invaluable.

2. GPS Paradigm in JVs

Unconventional Partnerships

Ground intelligence   Strategic solutions

As mentioned in the earlier chapters of M&A, even JVs and alliances would need to follow the GPS Paradigm. Hence, I thought this book must also include the basics of JVs to give the reader a fair idea of the intricacies of the subject matter. JVs and alliances, like M&As, are equally critically modes of business combinations. There are multiple forms of JVs, and it is necessary for us to dwell into those forms and structures as the **GPS Paradigm cuts across all forms & models of JVs in diverse industry sectors given that technology is the key driver.**

I repeat what I observed in the M&A section: there should be no doubt in the minds of business leaders and professionals working on M&A and JVs that the GPS Paradigm is the defining fabric of the next progression of the globalized tech-driven business world. A thorough study of different models of JVs and the peoples and processes involved in conceptualizing, initiating, and implementing any joint venture or alliance is imperative to understand how the GPS Paradigm would cut across them.

An insightful 2004 Harvard Business Review article brought to light several challenges facing JVs, which the authors rightly contend, made their prevailing JV success rate rather elusive. The prime reason for the lacuna, they believed, was the lack of planning preceding launch and execution which give birth to a litany of ensuing thorny issues, including erroneous strategies, incompatible partnerships, impractical deals, and susceptible management. Nothing much has moved since then, and many JVs across the globe largely suffer on the same counts barring exceptions. The GPS Paradigm is hence integral to the JV's sustainable success.

M&As and JVs Distinguished

Unconventional Partnerships

Ground intelligence   Strategic solutions

Conceptually and structurally M&As and JVs are two different methods of business combination to stay relevant, achieve growth and, if possible, dominate the market. We have seen key definitions and various forms of M&As, and the processes adopted to implement them. Since formation of a joint venture is more contractual in nature and not strictly governed by any legislative process or supervised by the courts like in the case of M&As, I have elaborated my experience of structuring JVs citing live examples. However, as I have constantly repeated in this book, any manufacturing or service industry would be severely affected by the advent of future technologies going forward. The trigger would be disruptive or breakthrough innovation, and the survival would depend upon the ability of the business leaders or decision makers to work keeping in mind the GPS Paradigm: of seeking **Ground Intelligence**, being flexible to build **Unconventional Partnerships**, and demonstrating the ability to deliver **Strategic Solutions**.

Start-ups eat, drink, and breathe the GPS Paradigm in some form or the other. That is their DNA! The prime reason for the staggering rise of unicorns is evident – they are not afraid to experiment. In fact, unknowingly, most of them have walked the path of GPS Paradigm. There is a lot to be learnt from their thought process and attitude of doing business vis-a-vis the arid and academic working of MNCs and large family-owned corporations; many of them are struggling to survive, clearly due to their inability to follow the GPS Paradigm.

Given the aforesaid background, it is extremely important for business leaders and future technologists to investigate, study, and analyze **ground intelligence** (with military precision as described in the earlier chapters) of evolving industry paradigms, advent of future technologies, shifting customer preferences, and potential strategic solutions of geographical deviations. Since today's competitors may well become tomorrow's natural allies or dependent partners, it is necessary to spend quality time on getting in-depth, 360-degree ground intelligence with credible and convincing forcefulness. It is the intricate and incomprehensible quality intelligence that would drive any new proposition, without which any aspirational growth is a non-starter!

Along with robust ground intelligence, it is important to design and forge **unconventional partnerships**; for example, partnering with technological platforms or gen-next product or services which may be totally unconnected with the original business model. 'Unconventional' here means not bound by convention: being out of the ordinary, not in conformity with what is generally done or believed, and what may take the world by surprise. It is high time the traditional industry veterans in agriculture, construction & engineering, consumer, healthcare, education, manufacturing, services, media & entertainment, fashion, banking, insurance, and the like integrate or tweak their business models in line with new customer preferences and technology platforms to connect their customers, vendors, and investors in more enduring ways than before.

The fundamental difference between M&A and JV is crystal clear: in case of M&As, the transferor company is merged into the transferee company and loses its existence. A Joint Venture on the other hand can be unbundled or unscrambled without much damage to the original business construct and allows the respective founders to continue as before. Of course, a robust JV merits proper design and articulation of the contractual rights and obligations in the agreement.

I would urge the next generation business leaders and decision makers to appreciate the robustness of the GPS Paradigm in the specific context of the flexibility of structuring a joint venture. If they touch the core of the GPS Paradigm, they will find a foolproof road map, a gen-next theory for business growth in the form of the GPS Paradigm. Each such JV would become a new structure for revenue or profit sharing, but over a period of time, it could get standardized in the given segment. **This awesome flexibility makes the GPS Paradigm an organic template for JVs across all revenue models – whether based on adverting, e-commerce, affiliate marketing, subscriptions, licensing, user data, sponsorships, donations, mobile and gaming, freemium, or virtual goods.**

The key to success here is to go beyond the backward or forward integration of business, or by executing traditional or copy book JVs.

The GPS Paradigm warrants a totally different approach towards setting up JVs based on ground intelligence, namely (a) identifying the partner who may be unconventional, (b) adopting novel revenue module, and (c) for inventing strategic solution.

Already, on the consumer side, we are seeing the emergence of unconventional and radical preferences that are forcing corporates to tweak or transform their business models with alacrity and acumen, or else get ready to face the perils of a difficult survival headed towards extinction. **Remote learning and working, online delivery and entertainment, shared mobility, and telemedicine are no longer an option, they have become the new normal in the COVID-19 era and even beyond. The new business models are increasingly focused on wellness-centric product development and innovation, close-knit digital communities, innovative shopping experiences, unique ways of customer engagement, intelligent brand mix, and on-the-go consumption avenues.**

Before we move to examine Classic JVs, it would be useful to to study the different forms of JVs with the help of real-world examples.

1. **Virtual Operator Model:** An operator company does not invest in proprietary physical assets; instead, it rents capacity from an integrated owner-operator company. For example, the virtual operator can purchase bulk network capacity from an integrated telecom carrier while retaining a separate commercial identity. The integrated carrier gets incremental revenues from its excess capacity. The model can be a win-win as long as the two companies address different customer segments. For example, Lycamobile, a big mobile VNO, focuses on expatriate communities looking for low-cost international pay-as-you-go calls in over 20 countries (Sector: Telecommunications)

2. **Asset Capacity Pooling:** Two companies that own and operate similar assets pool the capacity of their respective assets.

This model boosts utilization. In 2015, Maersk and MSC, the world's two largest liner-shipping companies, established 2M, a 10-year vessel sharing agreement covering 193 vessels. Given their complementary shipping schedules, services, and vessels, the agreement allows them to provide greater product options to customers at substantially lower operating cost. According to Maersk, the transaction led to production of an increased average vessel size, lower costs, better fee deployment, reduced gaseous emissions, and an annual benefit of $350 million. (*Sector: Shipping*)

3. **Joint Venture of Similar Assets:** Two companies transfer selected similar assets into a joint venture in order to support the orderly management of capacity in their industry and reduce the risk of a downward price spiral. This model is especially relevant when overall demand is declining, chronic overcapacity looms large, but continual investment in new technology is key amid uneven capacity investment. **Examples:** In 2010, Corelio and Concentra, two European media companies, established Coldset Printing Partners, a joint venture for their newspaper printing assets. In the meantime, the joint venture has also started doing contract printing for third parties. It is now the largest newspaper printer in Belgium, as of 2020. (*Sector: Media*)

4. **Joint Venture of Complementary Assets:** This is a joint venture riding on complementary assets and capabilities. This model limits upfront investments, speeds up market entry, and reduces risk. It is a powerful business consolidation tool. Ageas, a large European insurance company, has been using this model for its successful expansion into Asia. Ageas contributes its expertise in insurance product design, marketing, finance, and risk management, while the partner, often a well-embedded local financial institution, contributes its customer portfolio,

distribution channel, brand, and relationships. *(Sector: Insurance)*

5. **Dual Asymmetrical Joint Venture:** A long-term financial investor (company A) and an industrial operator (company B) set up two joint ventures for an industrial asset: one that owns the asset, and another that operates the asset. Company A has a majority stake in the owner joint venture and a minority stake in the operator joint venture, and vice versa for company B. This set-up provides company A with a steady dividend while allowing company B to reduce up-front capital outlays. The global energy player ENGIE and its local partners applied this model in the independent power production business in the Middle East. (*Sector: Energy*)

6. **Co-Funding of a Third-Party Asset:** Two companies co-fund a third party building an asset, often in exchange for exclusive or preferential access to part of the capacity. This model ensures access to an asset with decreased compliance. In 2012, Intel, TSMC, and Samsung — three large semiconductor manufacturers based in the U.S., Taiwan, and South Korea respectively — agreed to fund a novel technology development program at ASML, a leading equipment manufacturer based in the Netherlands. They also took an equity stake in ASML of 15%, 5%, and 3% respectively. The program banks on risk sharing, and the results of ASML's development programs will be available to every semiconductor manufacturer without restriction. (*Sector: Technology*)

7. **Joint Takeover of an Asset:** Two companies jointly invest in the takeover of a pricey asset, and subsequently benefit from its joint use. By doing so, they share the investment burden, reduce the lead time to build the asset from scratch, and possibly prevent the asset from falling into competitor hands. In 2015, a consortium of German car manufacturers Audi,

BMW, and Daimler took over Here – the digital mapping and location-intelligence business of the Finnish communications technology firm Nokia – on equal interest basis. According to BMW, the transaction would secure the company and enable it to serve industries independently, creating an open, independent and value creating platform for cloud-based maps and other mobility services accessible to all customers from the automotive industry and other sectors. (*Sector: Automobiles & Technology*)

Joint Venture as a Tool for Restructuring: Companies can use joint ventures as a tool to exit from non-core businesses, or ailing businesses that will lose value by being put up for sale. The model unlocks imprisoned assets, stakeholders stay committed, minimizes the burden on management, and due diligence and technical input during the restructuring is beneficial to the buyer. When Philips sought to reorganize its diverse portfolio in the late 1980s, it identified the $1.55 billion major domestic appliances division as not essential to its future. In 1989, Philips offered Whirlpool 53% of its appliances business for $381 million along with an option to buy the remaining 47% within three years. Whirlpool found the arrangement very attractive: It provided the company with an opportunity to learn about the reality of the appliance division as an insider and to initiate improvement plans before taking over the division entirely. For Philips, the joint venture provided the opportunity to prove to Whirlpool that the business really was as valuable as it claimed. Whirlpool exercised its option in 1991, purchasing the remaining 47% share for $610 million, and Philips exited the business smoothly and on substantially more favorable terms — the uplift was estimated at $270 million. (*Sector: Appliance Manufacturing*)

3. Classic JVs

Let us now examine the classic JVs and their instinctive adoption of the GPS Paradigm, though not in a conscious fashion:

1. **Pfizer-BioNTech (Year: 2020, Sector: Pharmaceuticals)** – This joint venture was announced to develop the first COVID-19 vaccine to achieve global authorization for emergency use. The same would consist of supply of about 50 million vaccine doses globally. **This is one of the best models of a complementary and timely joint venture which could save lives of millions, since BioNTech would be involved in producing mRNA supply for the vaccine whereas Pfizer would be involved in cold chain shipping, and supply and storage of vaccine in distribution centers worldwide.**

   This vaccine is the first to achieve emergency global usage authorization. Congratulations to the leaders of both BioNTech and Pfizer for their visionary steps in the right direction. I find this case an exceptional deployment of the GPS Paradigm, true in letter and spirit. I am sure both parties are already working towards combining their strengths to stay ahead of the curve in developing a ready-to-deploy framework for quickly countering future global calamities or contingencies similar or worse than COVID-19.

2. **Blockgraph (Year: 2020, Sector: Streaming & Media)** – This JV brought together three broadcasting giants – Comcast, ViacomCBS and Charter Communications, agreeing to take equal ownership of Blockgraph, an industry initiative and software platform designed to create a more secure way to use aggregated and anonymized data, and share information. **This joint venture is focused on ushering in a new way of using audience data for advanced TV and premium video advertising. Using Blockgraph technology, media companies can help marketers form insights across their collective platforms without relying exclusively on third parties. This is yet another classic example of the GPS Paradigm wherein the partners have innovatively used their strengths for mutual benefits.**

As per the joint venture's official press release, Blockgraph allows for these media giants to reshape data driven advertising in a more sustainable and confidential way. It would maximize data advertising in a secure manner, and thus benefit content providers as well. Going forward, they may even analyze audience data to create wholly new revenue models for them.

3. **Air Arabia Abu Dhabi (Year:2020, Sector: Aviation)** – A joint venture company of two leading airlines, Etihad and Air Arabia, the same was announced to act as a low-cost passenger airline with Abu Dhabi International Airport as its hub. The airline stated operations with two Airbus A320 aircraft based at Abu Dhabi International Airport.

    This is a highly effective method of combining complementary assets and skills in the form of a joint venture. As per Air Arabia CEO Adel Ali, despite coronavirus-based restrictions, the joint venture was said to be "working well", since it provides a low-cost option for short and medium haul passengers, which has not been drastically impacted by the Middle East coronavirus situation. In all probability, the current pandemic and the ground intelligence (GPS Paradigm) of economic downturn across geographies, which may stay put for some time, may have prompted the two airlines to play to their strengths in catering to the market demand.

4. **Volvo-Daimler (Year: 2020, Sector: Automotive Technology)** – This joint venture at a cost of the Volvo Group acquiring 50% of the partnership interests in Daimler Truck Fuel Cell GmbH & Co. KG, for approximately EUR 0.6 billion on a cash and debt-free basis was announced to develop, produce and commercialize fuel-cell systems for use in heavy-duty trucks as the primary focus, as well as other applications. This is a joint venture formed by co-funding another asset, in this case Daimler's subsidiary.

Seemingly, the ambition of both partners is to make the new company a leading global manufacturer of fuel cells, and thus help the world take a major step towards climate-neutral and sustainable transportation by 2050, and the transaction is expected to close by early 2021. I would term this as a copybook GPS Paradigm approach as outlined in this book. The success of the fuel-cell systems may give both partners access to other industries and even leadership position in automobile industry or any industry dependent on fuel-cell technology.

5. **Microsoft-Walgreens (Year 2019, Sector: Healthcare)** – As part of the deal, Microsoft will become Walgreen's new cloud provider. The two would reportedly work on innovative solutions to lower healthcare costs. Walgreens will open 12 "digital health corners" in stores to sell health care-related gadgets. This is another example of complementary joint venture.

   The partnership will reportedly help Walgreens gain personalized data about their customers' health, which will allow pharmacists to give better, customized nutrition, and wellness solutions. The concept of forming an 'unconventional partnership' for finding 'strategic solutions' as per the GPS Paradigm forms the very basis of this JVs. The same would also help Microsoft counter tech giant Amazon's healthcare ventures and establish global dominance.

6. **IBM-Vodafone (Year: 2019, Sector: Technology)** – This strategic collaboration would provide clients with the open, flexible technologies they need to integrate multiple clouds and prepare for the next wave of digital transformation enabled by Artificial Intelligence, 5G, edge and Software Defined Networking (SDN). The JV's reliance on future technologies aimed at progression, not survival is evident, which is again

a classic case of the GPS Paradigm. Under the new venture, Vodafone Business customers will have immediate access to the full portfolio of IBM's cloud offerings, underpinned by IBM's deep industry expertise and open technologies. As part of the agreement, IBM will provide managed services to Vodafone Business' cloud and hosting unit, in an eight-year engagement valued at approximately $550 million (€480 million). This is also an example of complementary joint venture.

The core of this joint venture is to help companies across Europe and beyond deliver innovation faster towards achieving success in a digital world. Customers would benefit from optimization, automation and cognitive capabilities, which help them to run their business effectively in a cloud environment. Also, the new venture will co-develop new digital solutions, combining the strengths of Vodafone's leadership in IoT, 5G and edge computing with IBM's multi-cloud, industry expertise and professional services capabilities. The success of these types of JVs would set a great precedent for future technologists in other industries as well.

7. **Eon-Clever (Year: 2019, Sector: Automotive Technology)** – This is a 50-50 joint venture to install high-speed charging stations for electric vehicles. The 48 charging sites will be installed in Denmark, Sweden and Norway, and will be operated by the joint venture, along with access to third-party providers. This is a complementary joint venture purely based on future technology.

An increased uptake of electric vehicles across Europe will enable utility companies to sell more power. The stations will offer power of more than 150 kilowatts (kW), meaning mid-sized cars can fully recharge in 15-20 minutes. I reckon the success of JVs like this one is critical to help set a fine precedent for future tech wizards and start-ups working on similar lines.

Yet again, a classic case of the GPS Paradigm in approach and thought process.

8. **Adnoc – Eni, OMV (Year: 2019, Sector: Oil and Gas) –**

In a landmark deal worth $5.8 billion, the UAE's energy giant Adnoc sealed an agreement with Italy's Eni and Austria's OMV for selling 35% stake in its refining business. As per the deal, Eni and OMV will acquire a 20% and a 15% share respectively in Adnoc Refining, with the Abu Dhabi company owning the remaining 65%. OMV will pay around $2.5 billion while Eni will pay around $3.3 billion, giving Adnoc Refining an enterprise value of $19.3 billion. The three companies also agreed to establish a joint venture trading operation. This is a case of joint venture used as a restructuring tool as described above. The deal will expand Adnoc's access to European markets as the three companies will sell refined oil products globally. It would also increase global refining capacity significantly for its European counterparts.

Chapter 9

My Tryst with M&As and JVs

Don't believe what your eyes are telling you.
All they show is limitation.
Look with your understanding, find out what you already know,
and you'll see the way to fly.

– Richard Bach, author of Jonathan Livingston Seagull

When I returned from my business trip to London in February-end, 2020, little did I know that the world was about to face a catastrophe of unprecedented size and scale, a calamity that was to change our lives and livelihoods forever, in ways we would not have imagined even in our wildest nightmares. Come March 2020, COVID-19 formally announced its arrival. It was clear by then that this toxic virus was a ruthless predator intent on playing havoc, although it was acknowledged as a pandemic much later.

This abrupt home confinement was a unique experience for countless professionals like me – a mandatory sabbatical of introspection and intrigue – that was thrust on us without prior intimation by forces beyond our control. During this period of lull, when I was searching for 'everything' in the name of 'something', I came across a gem of a book in 'Jonathan Livingston Seagull' written by pilot-turned-barnstormer-turned-celebrated author Richard Bach. I have lost count of how many times I read this four-part book ever since.

It was perhaps the outwardly simple but magnificently profound message that deeply resonated with me. Bach, who is spiritually fixated on flying and aviation as his chosen transcendental themes, tells a poignantly inspirational story of a stary-eyed seagull named Jonathan Livingston Seagull who dares to dream of those very things his folks have dismissed as being futile and unwarranted. While his mates chase the boats lured by the prospect of savoring scattered fish scraps and littered breadcrumbs, Jonathan takes to the skies to practice the dedication and discipline of flying. His love for the skies comes with a heavy penalty: he is expelled from his tribe and made an outcast, but that doesn't deter him from soaring higher in the guiding light of two seasoned gulls. Jonathan returns to his people to share the art and science of flying and spread love against all odds, as instructed by his guru. Braving the initial resentment and flippancy of the natives, he imparts his experiential wisdom to a few aspiring gulls, helps them see the virtues beneath the veil, and leaves for new shores after the new flocks have become adept at flying. Towards the end of the parable, Jonathan is predictably converted into a god by his community, and most gulls spend most time in blind worship and ostensible devotion. Soon after, a few birds shun the confines of conformity and take to flying with the vigour it demands. But there's a gull called Anthony who is consumed by the apparent futility of life and decides to end his life. However, he is motivated to think otherwise in the nick of time by an enigmatic, angelic gull who appears from nowhere, and when asked for his name, only says, "You can call me Jon!" This suggestive end is so powerful in its metaphorical imagery and unpretentious sermon that sincere readers can't help but seek to discover the Jonathan Livingston Seagull in them and appreciate the relevance in respective lives.

Every time I read the book, I go back in time to recount the cherished milestones of my personal voyage of over 30 years —

my school and college time, graduation span, law college days, internship interview, initial days of practice, golden time spent with my seniors, and career highs and lows as a corporate M&A lawyer! I have knowingly and unknowingly identified with Jonathan Livingston Seagull, in contemplative hindsight, as I try to connect the dots of the proverbial line that has brought me to where **I find myself today. Like Jonathan, I have suffered the pangs of discontentment with the humdrum of life, the misery of isolation and helplessness led by the craving to chart an education and career of choice, the unconditional love and support from my mentors at every decisive juncture, the need to be grounded at all times, and the urge to give back to the community by sharing what I have learnt over the years, whether from my seniors or from sheer experience.**

Today, when I look back, I find great satisfaction in having delivered the lecture series on M&A and joint ventures over a span of more than two decades on diverse platforms – be it ILS Law College, Pune, other law schools, or various fraternity meets.

However, I have experienced a deeper sense of fulfillment in the articulation of my home-grown experiences and insights, in the form of a new corporate theory titled 'GPS Paradigm', to help existing and future business leaders and decision makers deal with the diktats of disruptive technology and perpetual unpredictability in the course of designing and implementing their M&A and JV plans.

I sincerely hope my book helps founders, business leaders, CEOs, professionals, and students (of Law in particular) to make a positive difference through their contribution in the living waters of business – either as practitioners or consultants. This book is for those mavericks who, more than merely driving the change, are aspiring to **be the change.**

My Journey as M&A Lawyer

In a gentle way, you can shake the world.

– Mahatma Gandhi

Family upbringing and formative education play a vital role in shaping one's personal and professional development. In my case, the playground of life together with the classroom of my alma mater have provided me with a rich ammunition of actionable insights, which have proved handy in sustaining and celebrating many an umpteen trial and triumph of my corporate law career. I almost feel duty-bound to share a few pages of my life book before I come to charting the trajectory of my law career in the specific context of M&As, joint ventures, and collaborations. I am more than sure that budding professionals across different spheres will find my experiences handy in charting their own careers, through a conscious resolve to learn from the bagful of lessons that I have learnt over the years: the blunders that could have been nipped in the bud, the things that I did right, as also the umpteen trials and triumphs of my career as a corporate lawyer.

I am a first-generation lawyer. Before me, no one from my family had anything to do with law. Somehow, I always wanted to become a lawyer since my school days. Maybe I would have loved to become an architect, although I have thoroughly relished my career as a corporate lawyer.

Highs and Lows of Early Life

On the 21st day of February, 1963, exactly three months after the end of the Sino-Indian war, I was born to a good middle-class family in a locality inhabited by the Kutchi people (an enterprising business community widely spread across the globe). **I fondly remember my school, Sampson English High School run by Mrs. Sampson (principal), an Israeli lady known for her upright behaviour and hard discipline. Among other things, she taught us the significance of time, dress code, respect, and cleanliness.** Thanks to her, these core values have stayed with me till date. I am deeply pained if, for whatever reason, I am unable to make it to a meet at the scheduled time, or if I am not immaculately dressed up in line with the given occasion.

From the age of 14 till the time I completed my graduation in law, I became financially independent in my own right, managing my fees and personal expenses by giving tuitions to small kids. The irony of this whole affair was striking: At the age of 15, in the last year of school, I earned a princely sum of Rs. 750 per month. In stark contrast, after seven years, when I became a law graduate at 24, I fetched a meagre Rs. 500 per month as internship stipend. This is an extremely unfortunate reality of the legal profession in India. The scene is yet dismal in the legacy law firms though most new firms now pay a decent amount as internship.

It's high time Indian law firms adopted a basic minimum pay besides improving the apprenticeship working conditions through a structured and practical syllabus. In fact, given the COVID-19-imposed lockdown, online internship programs must be allowed to run parallel to conventional education, not just for law students but for probationers across engineering, architectural, accounting, and all other professions which put a premium on experiential learning.

Science to Economics: A Wanton Winding Route

I must share a monumental blunder of mine that happened at a crucial stage of my life. **In career, one is expected to take a right turn invariably and occasionally even turn left, but there are times when one should have the courage to take a U-turn if one approaches a dead end. The right path, no matter how long it takes to embark on it, will more than make up for the time lost — that is my assurance to all aspirants, regardless of the career stream.**

Since science was then considered a better for career in computer science, I opted for the science stream post matriculation. Honestly, I was keen on taking up commerce because it was the most logical route leading to a graduation in law.

My tryst with science met the expected fate. I cleared XI and XII class exams to join the Ramniranjan Jhunjhunwala College, Ghatkopar, for my graduation in Science. I knew this is not what my calling was, but I let the conundrum grow to alarming proportions. Initially, I took

Physics and Biology as my major subjects but later changed it to Physics and Math to escape the rigors of Biology practicals. After suffering an agonizing six months, I reached the boiling point beyond which I could take no more. I was downright depressed but had no idea whom to approach for advice.

Just about that time, some of my friends were pursuing graduation in Arts from the renowned Ramnarain Ruia College of Arts, Matunga. Almost led by instinct, **I decided to follow suit and enrolled for graduation in Arts (Economics & Politics). I also opted for Rural Development (RD) as an optional subject to get glimpses of rural India.**

The decision proved landmark for me as I got invaluable insights into rural life and Indian villages. In fact, at the age of 56, I completed my two years of Master's in RD. I may now pursue my PhD in Rural Development.

Coming back to my career, I swiftly completed my graduation in Arts with Economics and Politics as my major subjects. All waywardness was now behind me and I took up my law studies with great enthusiasm and renewed vigour.

Hardship and Articleship Hand-in-Hand

I studied law at the well-known Government Law College, Churchgate, Mumbai. Established in 1855, it holds the distinction of being the oldest law college in Asia. Most of my Ruia friends, probably in yet another play of destiny, wanted to become lawyers and solicitors. The peer pressure proved positive in my case as it was exactly about what I, too, wished to pursue.

I enjoyed my Law college time and particularly fancied 'contract law' which was taught by my Principal, Mrs. Advani. In a cruel blow of fate, I failed in that very subject in the first year of LLB. Thankfully, I was declared passed on revaluation as the examiner had not assessed an entire supplement of my paper. However, I lost one semester (six months) due to the revaluation, needlessly lagging behind my friends. That was the first massive setback in my legal education. I rejoined college, determined to begin my career as a lawyer as soon as possible, but deep within, I was totally dejected.

Hence, the day I cleared my second year LLB in October 1988, I rushed to call M/s. V. A. Phadke & Co. (a mid-sized law firm). I knew no one there, yet I called them up and spoke to the telephone operator, Mrs. Oak. Luckily, she happened to be a soft spoken, compassionate lady. I asked her about joining as an articled clerk. I still don't know why but she immediately reassured me with unexpected warmth, "Yes, why not? Please come and meet Mr. V. A. Phadke, we have a lot of students working for us."

Next day at sharp 10, I was at their office. Mr. Phadke, an upright man probably in his 70s, looked at me and shot out a flurry of questions in a rather dismissive tone: "Who are you? Who gave you my name? Do you have any reference? What do you know about my firm?" I told him I do not have any reference as I am the first-generation lawyer. Then, I gave him a very little background about myself.

He asked me to wait outside his cabin and I continued to wait all day. Around 5.00 pm, Mr. Phadke came out of his cabin and was about to leave when his eyes fell on me. My heart beat increased. He asked, "Are you still waiting? Did I not speak to you?" When he learnt that I had been waiting for that long, he seemed a bit apologetic and assigned me to work under Mrs. Kanta Aiyer, in litigation. That was how my articleship began. In fact, I had no regular workspace in office, so Mr. Phadke asked me to operate from the library. I was truly delighted as it gave me the freedom of reading any book anytime. Mrs. Aiyer was a Gujarati married to a Tamil chartered accountant. I was proficient in Gujarati which helped establish a very cordial working relationship, and I quickly learnt the ropes in her practice area. This experience gave me a ringside view of civil and property litigation, besides corporate work. I was very happy attending the celebrated Bombay High Court and the City Civil

Court where I successfully handled a range of litigations including one matrimonial matter. That was indeed the golden period in the history of the Bombay High Court. Every day, I was at the office at 9 am sharp. By 11, I used to complete all routine work before rushing to the High Court for listening to arguments of senior counsel stalwarts like Ram Jethmalani, Fali Nariman, Soli Sorabjee, Arvind Sawant, Bhimrao Naik, and D. R. Dhanuka (the last three eventually became celebrated High Court judges). I soaked in their wisdom wrapped in every word they used. I recollect having witnessed the trial of Shiv Sena supremo Shri Bal Thackeray before Justice Bharucha where Ram Jethmalani and Adik Shirodkar argued for Shiv Sena on an election challenged on the issue of Hindutva. I also attended the Harshad Mehta hearings (Securities Scam of 1992) before the Special Court of Justice Variava.

Solicitor's Exam: My Four-Year Penance

I always had a burning desire to learn as many different subjects as possible, and that is the reason I always see myself as a student. Probably that is also the reason that, years later, I did my Master's in Rural Development at the 'tender' age of 56! During graduation, I was happy to explore the depths of Economics, Politics and Marathi, ditto whilst learning 'Contract Law' at the Government Law College.

I passed law in 1989 but it was my keen desire to study law in depth, a yearning that was greatly satiated by my four attempts to clear the Solicitors Exam in May 1991.

I always knew that the Solicitors Exam was extremely tough, what with a passing percentage of 3 to 4%. Although the passing marks for each subject is 50%, one needs an average of 60% in the five subjects taken together to clear the exam. A preparation time of at least six months is an absolute must. In my first attempt, I failed to secure the aggregate by 11 marks! But I had no regrets as I thoroughly enjoyed studying for the second attempt as I got to see my subjects – chapter by chapter and section by section – in a new light. Unfortunately, I again failed in the second attempt too, clearing only two subjects: Companies Act and General Acts (open book exam). In my third attempt, I failed by a mere three marks in aggregate, but by this time I was on the verge of giving it all up. I just did not have either the strength or the inclination of studying all over again.

This was easily the most depressing span of my career when only a handful of people encouraged me to stay put. It is indeed unfortunate that one has to struggle all the way to find a beacon of guiding light, someone who is expected to do simple things like merely encouraging you not to give up. This was also the time I entered into wedlock. My wife Deepti was a pillar of strength and support during these tough times, so was my father. Also, my inner voice told me I was almost there, so I should not be giving up. I shared my predicament with Raju Shah, a senior Solicitor (also ex V. A Phadke & Co). He told me once I cleared the exam, the number of attempts will not matter. It was my father's gospel, wife's support, Raju Shah's encouragement, and my own tenacity that helped me touch the finish line. I distinctly remember I was in the courtroom of Justice Sujata Manohar when my court clerk barged in and conveyed the good news.

I would like to emphasize one point for the benefit of young lawyers, chartered accountants, engineers, architects, or for that matter any consultant: you may possibly have to change your path depending upon where your passion lies. Never lose heart. It may take some time to zero in on the right direction, but once you get on the right path, give it all you have! Always remember: your core knowledge, skills, and experience alone are your key working tools. Hence, you must strive to get quality education, ideally a coveted degree from any good university or institution, followed by credible work experience under a veteran. Enjoy the learning process with an open mind, even if it would eat into the initial years of your career. The blend of a good degree and an experienced mentor are an absolute must during your formative years. You reap what you sow! Your determination, tenacity, and commitment to your chosen sphere will together make all the difference.

Crawford Bayley Chronicles: Rich Reservoir of Actionable Insights

After conquering the exam front came the time to take the plunge into employment. By that time, I had identified Mr. R. A. Shah, Sr. Partner, Crawford Bayley (CB) as the topmost corporate lawyer of the country. I had made up my mind to work under him, but by the time I could apply, there was no vacancy at his office as someone else had already joined him.

With great difficulty I was able to join joinSenior Partner of CB, S. Y. Rege, in the litigation department, marking my entry in CB. That debut year at CB proved extremely frustrating: while Mr. Shah's juniors did plum corporate work, I was doing musty litigation that had reached the final hearing stage. This was a cumbersome process as I had to first dust old files and then struggle to read the old correspondence to understand the matter and then brief counsel to prepare them for hearing. **Every day, I was dying bit by bit under the weight of the monotony and rigor. This was the second biggest setback to my career, and I had no idea when the turmoil would end, and when my career would take off in the true sense.**

I was on the verge of giving up on my dream of becoming a corporate lawyer. With great reluctance, I had even forced myself to apply at Godrej Soaps for the post of legal manager. During the interview, the incumbent legal manager, a wise man, patiently heard me out before advising me to practice some old-fashioned patience and continue with CB. He reckoned I must give CB some more time since it was a good law firm. Enthused by his comforting words, I decided to continue my litigation work at CB.

Within a year's time, I was rewarded for my patience. As soon as I knew of a vacancy at Mr. Shah's chambers, I switched over without second thought, and Mr. Shah also readily accepted me. This transfer marked the turning point of my career. **Working with Mr. Shah was an awesome experience. Even today, at this juncture of my career, I would give an arm and a leg to work as his junior:** attending client meetings, taking instructions from him, discussing different law propositions, conducting research and analyzing legal propositions, preparing notes for his speeches, and simply observing him at work: his phenomenal patience, excellent listening skills and polite expression at any meeting. His drafting style – whether for letters or opinions – was simple, precise, and purposeful. He was always respectful towards everyone; always positive, proactive, and polite in all conversations. The individuals he interacted with comprised the who's who of law and business, including Nani Palkhivala, Ratan Tata, Nusli Wadia, Ajay Piramal, K. K. Modi, and many luminaries from abroad. As a highly competent lawyer, he had the uncanny ability to gauge the crux of the subject matter within no time, as also offer a 50,000-foot view for the benefit of the given audience. **His ability to stay objective and probe the root of any issue was incredible! Needless to say, he was extraordinarily brilliant in finding the most amicable solution, a win-win for all concerned parties. He was, and is, the Trusted Advisor of choice for many industrialists, professionals, and decision makers!**

Business Value of Linguistic Skills

As mentioned earlier, my knowledge and fluency of Kutchi (Gujarati) connected me deeply with many renowned Gujarati businessmen in India, including the Shahs (founders of Anchor) and the Chudgars (founders of Intas Pharmaceuticals), besides senior finance professionals and chartered accountants like Shailesh Haribhakti, Gautam Doshi, Bansi Mehta, and Arun Gandhi. How I wish I had learnt the German language back in the 1990s when I started working with Mr. Shah in Crawford Bayley. Somehow, Germany has been a key focus geography for me, given esteemed clients like Bayer, BASF, Siemens, Fresenius Kabi, Hannover Re, and many others. I would like to strongly recommend young lawyers or other consultants working with international companies to learn at least one foreign language, be it German, French or Japanese. Knowing the language of a given country opens its business doors in unimaginable ways, bestowing a phenomenally huge advantage!

The Big Leap of Liberalization

In July 1991, the then Finance Minister of India, Dr. Manmohan Singh, announced the new industrial policy which allowed foreign ownership in 34 industries to be raised to 51% from 40%. The Narasimha Rao government also allowed licensing of technology to Indian companies under the automatic route. This decisive step marked the beginning of a new era for Indian corporates. Mr. Shah was on the board of around 60 multinational companies (MNCs), primarily advising them on how they should raise their ownership stakes in India in the new Foreign Direct Investment (FDI) regime. Consequently, companies like Coca-Cola (and PepsiCo) returned to India in 1993.

It may be recalled that Coca-Cola was the leading soft drink brand in India until 1977 when it left India after the government ordered the company to dilute its stake in its Indian unit. It is pertinent to note that the government had earlier forced foreign companies to reduce their ownership to 40% under the Foreign Exchange Regulation Act, 1973 (FERA). At that time, the abysmally low foreign exchange reserves of the country were a scarce commodity. Later, under Dr. Singh's economic liberalization inititiave, the Government replaced FERA with the liberal Foreign Exchange Management Act, 1999 (FEMA) which allowed increase of ownership up to 51%, and even 100% in some select industries.

From 1992 till 1999, I represented the crème de la crème of Fortune 500 and top-notch companies under the visionary guidance of Mr. Shah. Our clientele included heavy weights like Colgate, Proctor & Gamble, Bayer AG, BASF AG, Boots Plc, Beiersdorf AG, Scholl Plc,

Gladerma, Unilever, Cadburys, Abbott, Fresenius Kabi, SmithKline Beecham, Amoco Corporation, Philip Morris, Roche, Rhone Poulenc, Allergan, Fiat, Seagram, Black & Decker, SKF, AkzoNobel, Givaudan Roure, Guinness Plc, Standard Chartered, AIG, the Tatas, the Piramals, RPG, Asian Paints, Bombay Dyeing, Britannia, and Atul Ltd.

M&A Deep Dive

We worked on highly innovative and intricate M&A and JV deals of listed and unlisted companies. We regularly got esteemed references from the likes of Ashok Wadhwa (who was then managing partner at Arthur Andersen), and investment banking firms like Udayan Bose (Lazard), Nimish Kampani and Adi Patel from JM Financial, Kotak (JV with Goldman Sachs), DSP Merrill Lynch, and many small Indian and overseas boutique firms.

During this period, I touched the depths of transaction tax and valuation — two key drivers of any M&A deal, from seasoned chartered accountants like Bansi Mehta, Arun Gandhi (NM Raiji & Co.), Dilip Doshi (C.C. Choksi & Co.), Y. H. Malegam (S.B. Billimoria & Co.), N. V. Iyer, not to mention senior partners from big accounting firms like Arthur Andersen, Coopers & Lybrand, Deloitte & Touche, Ernst & Young, KPMG and Price Waterhouse. Every interaction was illuminating and inspiring in the same breath.

Being the blue-eyed boy of Mr. Shah, he assigned me key international matters without second thought — such was his faith in me, and he invariably applauded my effort. **I soaked in the wisdom of this farsighted leader, studying his remarkable flexibility of approach without compromising his core, and his success mantra for difficult situations – of negotiating, conceding, compromising, and then crossing over.** He was a thoroughbred professional and very strict about meeting deadlines and keeping his word. These were the most potent working tools that Mr. Shah gifted me on a platter.

Thanks to the strong working relationships, many of my clients now shared a deep bond with me and considered me their trusted advisor. Notable among them were Ashok Chhabra & Deepak Acharya – both from Proctor & Gamble, K. V. Vaidyanathan of Colgate Palmolive India, M. R. Iyer of BASF, Gavaskar of Boots, Keval Handa of Abbott, Madhav Joshi of Bayer, C. B. Gagarani of Century Enka (Birla Group), and N. Santhanam of Bombay Dyeing.

Most of my work during this period was about setting up joint ventures, technical collaborations, mergers & acquisitions, demergers, as also business restructuring involving asset/business sale, succession planning, legal due-diligence and advising on exchange control regulations, and corporate advisory services to MNCs and their Indian affiliates and subsidiaries. We interacted directly with the key decision makers: the board members and top managements.

My first key M&A work under Mr. Shah was representing Colgate-Palmolive India Ltd in the $41.7 million acquisition of the oral hygiene business of Hindustan Ciba-Geigy, the Indian subsidiary of Ciba-Geigy A.G. of Switzerland (Ciba-Geigy). Hindustan Ciba-Geigy was 40 percent owned by Ciba-Geigy. Under the purchase agreement, Colgate took over Cibaca toothpaste and other brands, as well as the Ciba-Geigy's distribution and manufacturing arrangements. The purchase increased Colgate's share in India's toothbrush market to more than 70 percent. It was a great learning experience working with the M&A head of Colgate on how to structure the documentation for large and complex M&A transactions. His association gifted me with a treasure trove of invaluable insights. Mr. K. V. Vaidyanathan (Company Secretary & Legal Counsel of Colgate) was also extremely meticulous and equally supportive.

I was a regular visitor to the residence of the Chief Justice of India, late Y. V. Chandrachud, to seek his opinion on various corporate matters. I have lost count of the interesting courtroom stories I heard, straight from the horse's mouth. Those were the golden days of my early career.

I fondly recall the excellent working relation I had quickly established with late Rashmi D. Chandrachud (wife of SC judge Dhananjay Y. Chandrachud, son of late Y. V. Chandrachud). She represented Ciba-Geigy under the supervision of her senior, late Mr. Jangoo Gagrat, Senior Partner of Gagrat & Co., another reputed law firm in Mumbai. Mr. Gagrat and Mr. Shah were the best of buddies although they belonged to rival law firms. They shared their views with each other without the slightest hesitation. At the same time, they duly respected their professional boundaries. Unfortunately, I don't see that happening today with young lawyers even from the same law schools.

I fondly recall the string of Tata group assignments on which I worked very closely with Mr. Shah. In one key assignment, he was consulted by the Tata senior management on the unique **'TATA Brand Equity & Business Promotion (BEBP) Agreement" as they call it now. Essentially every company that uses the 'Tata' brand is a signatory to the Tata Sons' BEBP agreement. The agreement confers upon the operating companies the right to use the Tata brand in return for a commitment from them to run their businesses ethically and with excellence.** Mr. Shah during his early days in his career had extensively worked on matters concerning intellectual property, including trademark, patent, copyrights and designs; he had a thorough knowledge and understanding of the tenets of global brands/goodwill and reputation. Following the Tata Brand agreement, many other Indian groups also executed similar agreements to protect their respective brands.

My association with the Tatas continued even after my CB tenure, both during the Amarchand Mangaldas (AM) stint and the current stint at J. Sagar Associates (JSA). Notable transactions in the AM stint included the massive legal due diligence of the entire operations of Tata Consultancy Services Ltd., for their maiden initial public offering. TCS which started in 1968 had grown into one of India's largest and most profitable companies with an annual revenue of more than $1 billion. One of the Wall Street Journal's headline of the said time conveyed it all: **Big IPO in India Could Trigger Market Revival.** Later, in 2019, I worked closely with the senior management of TCS on the major reshuffle of key employees and other critical compliances.

I attended several professional meetings with Mr. Shah wherein there were a lot of learnings. Just to give a flavor: Once he had been asked by a large American Bank to seek the opinion of Mr. Nani Palkhivala (one of the greatest intellectual jurists of modern India) on the predictability of certain tax provisions in India. Mr. Shah had personally prepared the written brief, which Mr. Palkhivala had read in advance and was ready with his detailed notes. For over an hour, he gave us an overall picture of where the tax regime in India was falling short of international expectations, and what could be done to overcome that impediment. As a law student at Government Law College, I regularly attended Mr. Palkhivala' s annual lectures on India's Union Budget at the iconic Brabourne Stadium, Churchgate. However, the opportunity to be all ears to him in person, observing his humility and professionalism from close quarters, has been one of the biggest achievements of my professional career, which I will cherish all my life!

Paradigm Shifts in the SEBI Regime

The whole environment was electric as given the opening of the Indian economy, most foreign companies from the US & Europe sought to up their shareholding from 40% to 51% to acquire majority stakes in their Indian affiliates. This was the most opportune time for them to strengthen their market position by acquiring leading Indian companies and brands and consolidating their positions. The booming M&A market was at an all-time high.

On the one hand, the corporate landscape was changing rapidly, on the other, the Securities Exchange Board of India (SEBI) came into being, a watchdog to protect investor interest, promote the development of stock exchanges, and regulate stock market activities.

In 1994, SEBI came up with the first Takeover Regulations. Under Mr. Shah's guidance, I represented Bombay Dyeing which had made a competitive open offer for the Ahmedabad Electric Company (AEC), in response to the voluntary open offer made by Torrent Group to acquire AEC. This was the first-ever open takeover battle which severely exposed the SEBI takeover regulations. SEBI was forced to set up the Justice Bhagwati Committee (Ex Chief Justice of India) to review the takeover provisions, and Mr. Shah was invited to join as the committee member. Here again, I was fortunate to work closely and assist Mr. Shah to prepare the proposed amendments to the takeover code. SEBI had provided us with a lot of reading material, including Australian & UK codes which I studied in great detail. During that evolutionary phase of SEBI takeover regulations, we represented several companies who sought to defend hostile bids from Asian Paints, Saurashtra Cements, and the like.

Like Mr. Shah, I was invited as guest speaker by esteemed bodies like the Institute of Company Secretaries, Institute of Chartered Accountants, various stock exchanges, and law schools to unfold the essence of the SEBI takeover code, joint ventures & foreign collaborations, and mergers & acquisitions.

In what was my first truly independent assignment, I represented the Indian subsidiary of the German chemicals and pharma giant Bayer AG, which made an open offer to acquire ABS Industries Ltd (listed Indian company). This was the first time a foreign company made an open bid for an Indian firm following the enactment of the takeover code. This was a milestone deal as I had structured a first-ever and unique preferential allotment (primary issuance) of around 31% equity shares to Bayer and balance 20% via open offer, which was the mandatory size of open offer under the SEBI takeover regulations.

The Indian corporate world was thereby introduced to a novel structure for acquiring a listed company through a combination of issuance of fresh shares followed by an open offer from the public. As preferential allotment was exempt from the SEBI takeover regulations, the very acquisition of 31% stake rules out or frustrates the possibility of any competitive bid. I thoroughly relished working hand-in-hand with the M&A team of Bayer AG at Leverkusen, Germany.

Mr. Shah proudly acknowledged my contribution in designing this mode of acquisition. That was a watershed moment for me, for I had won accolades from the master for my professional acumen. In fact, in an informal chat, the then SEBI Chairman told Mr. Shah that this process was against the spirit of the SEBI takeover as it stifled the possibility of competing bids.

For Bayer AG, this acquisition was extremely important because ABS Industries was making acrylonitrile butadiene styrene, an engineering plastic used in various industries like automobiles, consumer electronics, and the luggage segment. Bayer has worldwide operations in acrylonitrile butadiene styrene, but none in India. This acquisition won Bayer a dominant share of the ABS market without investing heavily in a greenfield plant, a grand entry into India blessed with an enviable edge. What more could have Bayer asked for?

Based on the same strategy of issuance of fresh shares, we helped a family-owned cement company successfully defend a hostile bid. This was followed by a string of similar deals shielding companies against many a hostile bid.

JV Deep Dive

The most popular investment theme for the western world at that time was 'Destination India'. Every foreign company wanted to set up a joint venture or technical collaboration in India. On the other hand, many Indian entrepreneurs who visited the US or Europe hastily signed MoUs for setting up JVs in India. Majority of these MoUs were open-ended and allowed foreign companies to hold 51% equity ownership, precisely because the foreign companies aimed at consolidation and dominant control, given their superior technology & brand power.

However, over time, even 50:50 JVs were being signed, with one extra director to the foreign collaborator to enable consolidation. Consequently, many friendly JVs came into being. Where any conflict arose, the foreign players were ready for a compromise as they were eager to commence business in the goldmine that India was.

For me, the most interesting part of the negotiations were the provisions with regard to buyout clauses in the case of deadlocks, 50:50 shareholding, or exhaustive list of items requiring affirmative votes. Deliberating with Mr. Shah on the alternative structures to resolve conflicts or deadlocks proved a highly interactive and fascinating learning. Mr. Shah had lot of insights on the working of the Indian companies, their succession planning, and management styles. He was thus able to quickly recommend tailored mechanisms for deadlock resolution. Among these options, Russian Roulette was my favorite.

That structuring a joint venture is more a business decision than legal is something I learnt under the tutelage of Mr. Shah. We must have together structured over 100 JVs and multiple other forms of alliances for Indian and foreign companies operating in India. I had the complete freedom of suggesting equity, management structure, and deadlock resolutions. I distinctly recollect our representation on behalf of a large Indian hospital run by a very senior US-returned doctor. He was negotiating with a Private Equity (PE) investor to acquire a stake in his hospital. The PE investor had a veto on all critical items save for one. I had proposed that in the event of a deadlock the founder doctor should have the first right to offer to purchase and/or replace the PE investor at the 'fair price' decided by any independent valuer. My logic was rooted in the fact that the hospital was essentially an Indian venture. However, the PE fund manager stridently sought the right to counter and outbid. Mr. Shah intervened on behalf of the founder doctor and made it abundantly clear that if the proposal were not acceptable, he would find another investor who would allow the founder doctor to cherish his dream of serving his home country. Such was Mr. Shah's conviction that the PE investor finally gave his consent to the deadlock resolution.

Whilst discussing the basic structure of equity of 50:50 or 51:49 or any minority investment, Mr. Shah spent substantial time to understand the ownership structure, role of founders, their managerial capability, role of strategic partners, tentative business plan over the next five to ten years, and the way competitive businesses were positioned. He would counsel the founders to keep their expectations at reasonable levels. Because of his vast experience of working with MNCs operating in India, he knew how decisions were usually taken and proceeded with. At the same time, he was very closely associated with the Indian founders. He never advised any client to take advantage of any situation and was always fair, objective, and reasonable in recommending a prudent business decision without compromising on the commercial interests of both parties.

In what was an interesting case, two brothers of a large electronic goods company and liquor were fighting tooth and nail over ownership issues. We were representing the elder brother who was extremely furious, keen on kicking his younger brother out of business as the latter was siphoning off funds. Mr. Shah intervened and convinced him to make an amicable separation and thereby avoid bitter court battles, which would only be in the interest of lawyers from a purely financial perspective.

Inevitably, the Indian owners were averse to negotiation (or even discussion) on deadlock resolution clauses. In sharp contrast, the foreign companies were always open to a detailed deadlock resolution mechanism, including the final buyout provisions. We had to spend considerable time explaining to the Indian promoters that it is in their interest to have clarity on the way forward lest things do not materialize or if partners do not get along well. I recall a JV finalization between a large Indian house and an

MNC where the company chairman explicitly told us to keep the matter open and not provide any solution. Why? Because he was nervous about something going wrong even before the JV was signed.

Dizzying Career Highs

It was normal to provide that following the termination of the JV agreement, the party existing should not compete with the JV nor poach the key employees of the company. The big question was about the validity of such non-compete provisions particularly when the joint venture is in the form of a company. Lawyers were divided on this issue and a majority were of the view that this restrictive provision is against Section 27 of the Indian Contract Act, 1872, which declared that any agreement that restrains anyone from exercising a lawful profession or trade or business of any kind, is to that extent void.

I did some research on this topic and argued that under Section 36(2) of the Indian Partnership Act, 1932, it is legally permissible to restrict an outgoing partner from carrying on any business similar to that of the firm within a specified period or local limits, and this is notwithstanding anything contained in Section 27 of the Indian Contract Act, 1872. I relied on the jurisprudence of our Supreme Court which in several of its leading cases declared that joint ventures are quasi partnerships, and it is permissible to apply the principles of partnership for dissolution in such joint ventures. My opinion was widely circulated in corporate circles and accepted by majority of corporate lawyers whilst structuring joint ventures. (Refer the Supreme Court implications in the landmark judgment of Gujarat Bottling Case cited in the chapter on joint ventures).

One of my key representations, in the liberalization era, was Fiat SpA which had identified a huge potential in the Indian car market. I went to the Turin headquarters of Fiat in December 1996 at the behest of Mr. Scognamilio, the then General Counsel, to prepare and negotiate the technical collaboration with Premier Automobiles Limited (PAL).

As part of Fiat's World Car Project for emerging markets, the Fiat Uno vehicle was imported and assembled from completely-knocked-down (CKD) kits. Simultaneously, Fiat set up its wholly owned greenfield plant at Ranjangaon near Pune in Maharashtra for the production of its World Car model range.

This was the time when Maruti Suzuki had no competition in India. Maitreya Doshi, the Managing Director of PAL, was keen to develop a car to compete with Maruti, what with Hyundai already having announced its plans to set up a small car manufacturing plant in Chennai.

I also worked with a large Indian pharma group which got big during the 90s merely on the strength of a series of strategic M&As. The chairman had built quite a reputation for managing successful JVs with MNCs. His instructions to me were very clear: in case of any difference of opinion or dispute, let parties bid for each other's shares after determining the minimum fair valuation decided by any independent agency. The whole idea was focused on protecting the interests of the JV company, not the individual shareholders.

The AM Sojourn: My Tryst with a Family-Owned Set-up

Sometime in 1997 CB decided to add around six new partners and I consider myself fortunate to be named in the probable list. However, for reasons best known to the then partners of CB, we were not made partners despite announcing the date for our induction. We were all terribly disappointed and I had almost decided to quit the firm, when all of a sudden, I got a call from Cyril Shroff to join his law firm Amarchand Mangaldas & Suresh A. Shroff & Co. [as it was known prior to the split between Cyril Shroff (Mumbai) and Shardul Shroff (Delhi)]. In the first meeting itself, I struck a chord with Cyril and decided to join him. As an Amarchand Mangaldas (AM) partner, I continued my M&A work with the same vigor as before.

AM had been advised by external consultants to broaden their partnership and that is how I was identified by Cyril to join the firm. I must say that AM, though a family-owned firm, was totally committed to the goal of making the firm truly international in size and substance. At times Cyril was criticized for his autocratic functioning to which he had a matter-of-fact reply: "I am a benevolent dictator, and I do not want my firm to become a debating society."

Cyril was clear about the need to take quick decisions in the larger interest of the firm. I enjoyed an extremely cordial working relationship with Cyril and Shardul and their respective wives Vandana (an astute lawyer who maintains a firm grip over the admin support of AM Mumbai office) and Pallavi (a Delhi-based litigation & competition lawyer, and daughter of former Chief Justice of India P. N. Bhagwati), as also their mother late Bharti Shroff (herself a banking & finance lawyer). In 2014, almost nine years after I had left them, the family entity was split following the demise of Bharti Shroff. Now both Cyril and Shardul successfully run their own firms and have grown even bigger individually.

I was advised by colleagues against joining AM in 2000 because it was a family-owned and run firm, but I took a conscious call of joining Cyril as I really liked his dynamism. I had decided to give myself five years with AM but actually clocked in a year more. I had the freedom to run my M&A practice. Yes, had Cyril entrusted me with more responsibility, I would have probably stayed longer. I was keen to be part of the development process, particularly the IT infrastructure or knowledge management of the firm.

Both Cyril and Shardul are well-respected and well-networked names in the Indian corporate world. I am not aware of their working style post the split but would always remain their well-wisher.

My notable transactions in the AM stint included the massive legal due diligence of the entire operations of Tata Consultancy Services Ltd (as mentioned above). Following the success of the TCS IPO, I conducted the legal due diligence of UltraTech Cement – the cement division of India's largest engineering conglomerate, Larsen and Toubro Ltd (L&T), which was sold to the Aditya Birla Group.

Among other interesting cases during the AM tenure was the demerger and separation of the listed player, Duphar-Interfran, from Solvay Pharmaceutical Ltd. I extensively worked with Vishal Nevatia, Managing Partner of True North Fund (earlier known as India Value Fund), a homegrown private equity firm. I advised Sharavan Shroff of Shringar Films (largest film distributors in India) on their foray into the multiplex business in Mumbai. I also relished working with Gautam Saigal of AIG Global Investment Group (Asia) and Co-Head of India PE advisory practice.

The JSA Chapter: Pinnacle of my M&A and JV Voyage

AM was essentially a family-owned firm, so in due course I sought opportunities to work with a more egalitarian set-up. I joined

J. Sagar Associates (JSA) in October 2005, where I continue to work till date. **A truly merit-based and democratic law firm, JSA is structured just like any European or American law firm. It has an elected managing committee, and it offers partners complete freedom for practice based on mutual trust. The uniqueness of our firm is that we, by constitution, have agreed not to take any of our family members on board, only to steer clear of any bias, and we also have a compulsory retirement age of 65.** In fact, Jyoti and Berjis retired at 60! And the next generation leaders have successfully transitioned into playing bigger roles and also have now structured JSA into an institution. We have a fantastic battery of young promising lawyers who I am sure will do exceedingly well in their respective practice areas and take JSA to new heights.

I have continued my M&A and foreign investment work with even more enthusiasm in the JSA era. My work includes business restructuring, asset/share transfer deals, private equity, business succession planning, and general corporate advisory. I have built a team of good lawyers besides contributing to the growing list of esteemed clients. Somehow, my focus has remained on working for German companies like Fresenius Kabi AG, which I have serviced for over 15 years, including serving as an independent director on their Indian listed subsidiary. Transitioning to JSA was easy for me as I had worked with the chairman, Jyoti Sagar, in 1996 when I represented French Magazine ELLE and Jyoti represented Bhartia Group. I found Jyoti extremely polite and cordial during that interaction and this experience had actually sowed the seeds in my mind, of considering JSA as a prospective firm to partner with. In another coincidence, my first transaction as Partner of AM was against Berjis Desai (JSA Managing Partner, Mumbai) wherein I stood for AIG Fund for a private equity investment in a French company, Ethypharm, represented by Berjis. In the very first interaction, I had won the faith and trust of Berjis who gave me a free hand to negotiate on the investment documents.

The leadership of Jyoti and Berjis was accommodative, democratic, and respectful. They insisted we partners be always open and collaborative. In turn, all partners have strived to maintain the DNA of our firm, built brick by brick by Jyoti & Berjis. When I joined JSA in 2005, the firm had a total of 63 lawyers across three locations. Today in 2020, we are a big family of 330 lawyers – a perfect blend of senior and junior partners – spread across seven locations, including the office I started at GIFT IFSC, Ahmedabad in 2018 for a specific duration.

In all humility, I feel elated to mention that I have worked on many landmark and marquee transactions of the Indian corporate world. It would be pertinent to take a closer look at a couple of them, as also a few of the key litigations handled by me.

Anchor – Panasonic

Anchor Electricals, the 50-year-old, family-owned, top-notch brand was sold to Matsushita Electric Works (maker of Panasonic, Japan's No. 1 brand in electric equipment) for 50 billion yen ($420 million). I found the deal extremely interesting as I represented the entire family that owned Anchor and closely worked with them for close to nine months. I conducted a time-consuming and back-breaking vendor legal diligence of the entire Anchor operations prior to the negotiations and documentation. This effort was necessary because of the vast operations of Anchor spread across India which had to be consolidated from multiple smaller firms into one entity for ensuring ease of transfer. I am glad that Atul Shah, the Managing Director of Anchor, reposed total confidence in me to handle negotiations, documentation, and closure end-to-end. My Kutchi language proficiency again played a key role in strengthening the relationship as the Shah family belongs to the Kutchi community. Knowing their mother tongue made our conversations as seamless as possible. During the negotiations, I worked closely with the legal counsel, David Allen Tally, and several team members from Panasonic. The Panasonic team was extremely meticulous in its approach and the whole environment was very cordial and harmonious.

As a matter of practice, whenever I deal with a reputed brand, I study a little bit of its history, in particular the groundwork done by the founders. When I did an extensive research on Panasonic and studied their past acquisitions across the globe, I was more than confident that they would go all-out to acquire Anchor, the number one brand in India. Also, during informal conversations with their team, I sensed their deep aspiration of assuming numero uno position in any country. I subtly unfolded the Anchor success story for their benefit, how they became a trusted household name in India. This elaboration helped iron out many minor issues and eased the negotiations. I thoroughly enjoyed representing Atul Shah and his family members, and they continue to be my clients to this day.

Camlin-Kokuyo

I represented the founding family of Camlin, No. 1 in stationery products in India, when they sold their controlling stake to Kokuyo, No. 1 in paper products in Japan. The acquisition was structured as a combination of 10 per cent shares via primary issue, open offer for 20 per cent as mandated under the SEBI Takeover Regulations, and around 20 per cent from the founders. **Exiting the business was an extremely emotional decision for the family. Hence, I had structured the management transition in a phased manner which allowed the Dandekar family to cherish their position and reputation as one of India's leading brand makers.** Fortunately, the family reposed total confidence and faith in me for the negotiations that took place in Tokyo. My objective was to tick all the minimal but decisive commercial points towards ensuring an amicable agreement. Thanks to my studied approach and grasp over the subject matter, I stayed focused, assertive, and firm in my position end to end. And since I was single-handedly leading the negotiations, I had to act extremely tough on behalf of my client, which created an image, in the minds of the Kokuyo management, that I was an extremely aggressive lawyer. Having said that, during the concluding phase of negotiations, the Kokuyo management team wholeheartedly appreciated the steadfast manner in which I represented the Dandekar family. Right from the beginning, I was convinced about the certainty of this deal. Camlin did enjoy an enviable reputation in India as a stationery giant, but since the market was becoming ultra-competitive, I was confident that Kokuyo would offer best-in-class support to Camlin – whether in terms of raw material quality, best of breed equipment, R&D capabilities, or the financial muscle to infuse fresh capital.

2011 Tōhoku Earthquake

After three days of hectic negotiations in Tokuyo, I stayed back to meet a few reputed law firms in Tokyo. On my last day in Tokyo, on Friday the 11th of March 2011, I was in meeting with Mr. Ushijima, the founder of a local law firm, Ushijima & Partners. At 1.45 pm, Japan (Pacific Coast) was hit by an earthquake of magnitude 9.0–9.1. Mr. Ushijima's secretary, visibly shaken, entered our conference room and conveyed the news. I was on the 12th floor of Sanno Park Tower, and the lights went out. From the balcony, I recorded a short video on my mobile capturing the shuddering building and people running helter-skelter on the streets. Mr. Ushijima asked me if I was fine! I told him: if you are fine, I am fine! Anyway, after an hour or so, I had to climb down 12 floors to begin a one-hour walk to my hotel.

I later learnt about the horrifying enormity of the disaster. It was an undersea megathrust earthquake off the coast of Japan with an epicenter of approximately 70 kilometers east of the Oshika Peninsula of Tōhoku. Aptly called the Great East Japan Earthquake, or the 2011 Tōhoku earthquake, it was the most powerful earthquake ever recorded in Japan, and the fourth most powerful earthquake in the world since the advent of modern record-keeping in 1900.

I was astonished to note the patience and discipline that common people demonstrated on the streets of Tokyo. There were no metros, buses, or taxis plying on the road; people were quietly walking on the footpaths without the slightest anxiety or hassle. Since I had no clue of the directions, I had to frequently consult pedestrians. Many of them had small maps of Tokyo with them and were very proactive in helping me find my way back. My return flight having been cancelled, I called up home and informed my wife about my safety. I was in compulsory confinement in my hotel room for the next three days, watching and admiring Japan systematically responding to the disaster. People patiently queued up for water bottles and food packets. I came back to Mumbai with a successful deal and an earth-shattering experience of a lifetime...literally!

LIC Nominee Directors on L&T Board – Corporate Litigation

Whilst all my life I have practised as a corporate lawyer, I have also worked as a litigation lawyer for high profile matters. I distinctly remember that LIC (Life Insurance Corporation of India – India's state-owned largest personal insurance group and investment corporation) sought my advice on their corporate governance issues, particularly about their nominee directors on the boards of various LIC-invested companies. It had all begun with a Business Standard headline about two nominee directors of LIC having received employee stock options from Larsen & Toubro Limited (L&T), the well-known Indian conglomerate into technology, engineering, construction, manufacturing, and financial services that was founded by two Danish engineers. The stock options so granted were clearly in violation of the letter and spirit of the employee stock option regulations applicable for listed companies. Essentially, to be eligible for getting employee stock options shares, one must be in regular employment and not merely a nominee director of an investor, like LIC in this case.

LIC wanted to act against their own nominee directors, and my friend, Ms. Sadhna Dhamne, the Legal Counsel of LIC, approached me and asked me to take appropriate action. I immediately consulted Sr. Counsel Ravi Kadam of the Bombay High Court, and we moved the court to seek an injunction against the two nominee directors. I called up the Editor of Business Standard and informed him about the injunction order; the news was also widely reported by many other newspapers. Embarrassed by the media attention, the two nominee directors of LIC were all too keen to settle the matter amicably, which did happen soon after.

MCX-SX Stock Exchange

In another major corporate litigation, I represented MCX-SX, the equity Stock Exchange in India set up by my client Jignesh Shah (wo was named the Global Young Leader by the World Economic Forum in 2007). Somehow, the Securities and Exchange Board of India, the regulator of the securities and commodity market in India, was not in favour of granting permission to MCX-SX to open a full-fledged Equity Stock Exchange that would compete with the Bombay Stock Exchange and the National Stock Exchange of India. It was apparent the action of SEBI was patently wrong. We had to fight an extremely bitter court battle which went right up to the Supreme Court.

I also worked extensively for the Jignesh Shah-promoted Financial Technologies (FTIL) (now known as 63 moons technologies limited) which offers technology intellectual property to create and trade on financial markets. I helped FTIL set up and divest various exchanges globally including in Dubai, Singapore, and Mauritius.

GIFT IFSC

I worked extensively with the Management of GIFT IFSC for the Gujarat International Finance Tec (GIFT) City, Ahmedabad. GIFT City is India's first operational smart city and international financial services centre, comparable with financial centers in Dubai, Singapore, London, and Dublin. The integrated development covering 886 acres of land with 62 mn sq. ft. of built-up area includes office spaces, residential apartments, schools, hospital, hotels, clubs, retail and various recreational facilities, which makes this City a truly "walk to work" City. GIFT City consists of a conducive Multi-Service SEZ (Special Economic Zone) and an exclusive Domestic Area.

I had the opportunity of working closely with Ajay Pandey, Former Managing Director, and Dipesh Shah, Head – Development & International Relations, to structure various legislations, including the 50 key amendments to the Indian Companies Act, 2013 that offered certain special exemptions and benefits to companies set up in GIFT IFSC. Separately, I was instrumental in successfully setting up a collaboration between GIFT IFSC and Singapore International Arbitration Centre (SIAC) and also helped GIFT IFSC in structuring the establishment of International Financial Services Centres Authority, 2019 to regulate all financial services in GIFT IFSC. This unified authority would be headquartered in Gandhinagar, Gujarat providing a single window regulatory institution to accelerate the development of India's first IFSC.

Prior to the inception of this unified regulatory authority, the banking, capital markets, and insurance sector regulations in GIFT IFSC were being done by multiple agencies, namely the Reserve Bank of India (RBI), the Securities and Exchange Board of India (SEBI), and the Insurance Regulatory and Development Authority of Ind**ia (IRDAI) respectively.**

Addendum to My Corporate Work

My mainstream career took an unexpected turn on the completion of the landmark Anchor-Panasonic transaction (mentioned above). After the press conference, I was interviewed by the business correspondent of 'Loksatta' (a Marathi newspaper of the Indian Express group) Mr. Prasad Kerker on my role as a corporate lawyer in mega deals, India's foreign investment policies, and the trends of foreign investment in India. He insisted that **I write my experiences on joint ventures & foreign collaborations and various aspects of Entrepreneurship.** Pursuant to his request, I wrote around 20 articles between 2007-2010 on entrepreneurship, capital, innovations, foreign collaborations, human resources, marketing, branding, and trends. At the behest of Shri Kumar Ketkar (Senior Editor), I compiled these articles and published a book titled 'Pragaticha Expressway' on February 16, 2011. Soon after, in addition to my regular lectures on M&As and JVs for law students, I started sharing my experiences at various business forums, chambers, and management schools.

During these sessions, **I realized that entrepreneurship education and encouragement hold the key for the next generation.** Encouraged by the reception of my book, and responses to my business sessions,

I founded Maxell Foundation (www.maxellfoundation.org), a non-profit trust (2012-2017) conferring the Maharashtra Corporate Excellence Awards for felicitating and encouraging entrepreneurs, innovators, business leaders, and young start-ups from the State of Maharashtra. The advisory board comprised the who's who across diverse sectors: Dr Raghunath Mashelkar (India's premier scientist), Kumar Ketkar (Sr. Editor), Late Y. M. Deosthalee (Chairman & CEO of L&T Finance), Justice (Retd.) Arvind Savant, Sunil Deshmukh (Renowned commodity trading expert), Shailesh Haribhakti (Sr. Chartered Accountant), and Dinesh Keskar (Sr. VP, Boeing India). From 2012 to 2017, we conferred around 42 Maxell Corporate Excellence Awards to achievers across diverse sectors and spheres in grand annual ceremonies at landmark venues.

In the meantime, **I designed a short program titled 'Maxplore' for teaching entrepreneurship to school and college students wherein I shared the concept of '3-I: Introspect, Ideate and Implement'.** I published a short practical guide to develop entrepreneurial traits amongst school children which was released at the hands of Shri Rahul Bajaj (senior industrialist) at the Maxell Annual Awards – 2016. I personally took few pilot sessions on entrepreneurship for school and college students in Mumbai and Pune. It is still a work in progress! Sam Pitroda (father of India's Computer and IT Revolution) was the Chief Guest for Maxell Awards in 2017, who suggested that I do 'conversations' in lieu of the award functions so that people are able to share their insights and experiences. I deliberated on his suggestion with my advisory board, and we decided to terminate the Maxell Awards in 2017.

However, the idea of holding conversations stayed in my mind. Almost three years later, when the pandemic enforced a lockdown in March 2020, the concept and craze of 'Zoom' digital meetings had caught on. On the economic front, rightly or wrongly, while China faced a backlash from the international community for the spread of COVID-19, India caught the attention of global companies as an alternate manufacturing destination. **I swung into action and set up the 'India Power Talk' (www.indiapowertalk.com) – a digital platform (webinar series) assembling international leaders from diverse sectors to talk on economy, environment, and education. The idea is to create an easily accessible digital source of diverse business knowledge, which would benefit Indian entrepreneurs, international businesses, institutional investors, and strategic partners either active in India or intending to invest in the country.** The Indian Chamber of Commerce, Indo-American Chamber and LawSikho (largest online education portal) came forward to share their members as audience. I am happy that, in a span of 10 months, I have hosted around 18 distinguished guests who have shared their thoughts with me on various interesting subjects.

Music & Colours

In addition to my mainstream preoccupation, I have a keen interest in music and paintings since my school days. In fact, for the past two years I have been taking out time to learn playing the piano. Earlier I was a regular visitor to Jehangir Art Gallery at Kala Ghoda, Mumbai, to study the artwork of several artists, interacting with them, and grasping their artistic perspectives. I also took a few painting lessons from a few artists since 2016. Fortunately, I ended up joining hands with a few artists for a group show titled 'Odyssey' at Jehangir that was inaugurated by senior artist Prabhakar Kolte on June 19, 2018. **My paintings, titled 'Impressions', were an abstract interpretation of the world of law and its people based on my 30-year practice. My exhibition was very well received. Conceptually, my tryst with the canvas was no different from my tryst with law.**

The journey continues ...

Nitin Potdar

Key representations over the years	
Nissan Distribution (in their restructuring Indian operations)	Monash University, Australia
Clearwater Capital Fund	TOTAL SA, France
Kinetic Engineering	NTT Data Corporation, Japan
Cookie Man Australia for India entry	Resolution plc and Friends Provident plc
Pantaloon (Future Group) in their series of JVs, including Dixons UK, Lee Cooper UK, Liberty Shoes, ETAM, Future Capital	(in their global merger having impact in India)
	Tamasek Singapore
	T-Systems Enterprise Business Services GmbH
Robeco Group N.V., Netherlands (for setting up JV with Canara Bank)	(subsidiary of Deutsche Telekom AG)
	Springer Science + Business Media, Germany
Alteams Oy for setting up JV in India	Swiss Re, Switzerland
	Vertellus Specialities, US
Devgen NV, Belgium	Cementia Trading AG, Zurich
Ecom Agro-industrial Corp Ltd	Ecolab Inc, US
Associated British Foods Plc	Enics Group, Zurich
IFCI Ltd	Hitachi Automotive, Germany
Ecocert SA, France	Knorr-Bermse, Germany
FMO (the Netherlands Development Finance Company)	Petronas, Malaysia
	Fori Automation, US
HTC Sweden AB	Nissan Japan
Paracor Capital Advisors	Titan Cement Company S.A
Sportal Australia Pty. Ltd	Altana AG, Germany
Bayer HealthCare AG	Grundfos AG
Boehringer ingelheim	The Timken Company Inc, US
BP Energy	CDI Corporation Inc., US
Maxis Communications, Malaysia	Sony Corporation, US
Nisshinbo, Japan	DKSH
OFIC Onduline, France	LIC India
General Mills Inc, US	Wockhardt Ltd, India
Hannover Re, Germany	
Interserve Plc, UK	

Practical Tips for Law Students Aspiring to Become M&A Lawyers of Repute

It isn't where you came from; it's where you're going that counts.

– Ella Fitzgerald

- Study the provisions of all applicable laws in relation to M&A, including Companies Act, 2013, SEBI Takeover Regulations/Foreign Direct Investment Regulations (FEMA)/Competition Act, and allied rules & regulations. Prepare a detailed chart/notes on the legal process, key steps, legal due-diligence, and documentation — including term sheet, various types of M&A schemes & demergers along with a detailed timetable for implementing M&A (for both listed & unlisted companies). **Make exhaustive personal notes and a rich repository of reference material.**

- Study major court decisions dealing with various issues arising during M&As, including valuation, role of directors, dissenting & minority shareholders, creditors, employees, applicability of competition law/exchange control regulations, public policy, industry specific regulatory regime, common objections by regional directors, SEBI Takeover Regulations, income tax and the like. **Retain copies of important decisions with your own personal markings.**

- Study various models of JVs, documentation involved like MoUs, Share Purchase Agreement, Share Subscription Agreement, Shareholders' Agreement or Joint Venture Agreement and other Ancillary Agreements such as Trademark License Agreement, Marketing & Distributorship Agreement, Export Promotion Agreement, Manufacturing Agreement (also called as Toll Manufacturing), Technology Transfer or License Agreement, Agreement to Depute Technicians, Employment Agreements,

Agreement to Rent Office. **Collect drafts of these documents and diligently practice drafting these agreements.**

- Develop a habit of reading key business newspapers and magazines to track business news in India and globally across industries and service sectors. Read various articles, reports, analyses, and research publications on M&A from leading consulting companies like McKinsey/Bain/international universities like Harvard/Oxford/London Business School/Forbes. **Maintain newspaper cuttings/articles for future reference.**

- Write columns, articles, or research papers on topics on interesting topics in newspapers or post them on your social media. Regularly attend seminars/discussions as audience and seek speaker engagements on diverse subjects at your own law school, the Institute of Company Secretaries, Institute of Chartered Accountants and other key business chambers/forums.

- Develop close professional network of people from diverse fields, including Transaction Tax/Audits/Investment Bankers/Intellectual Property, Employment and Environmental Law Experts, Company Secretaries & In-house counsel. **Make a point to meet them regularly and hold discussions on issues.**

The only way to do great work, is to love what you do.

– Steve Jobs

www.ingramcontent.com/pod-product-compliance
Lightning Source LLC
Chambersburg PA
CBHW020905180526
45163CB00007B/2630